Biography

James Egan was born in 1985 and lived in Portarlington, Co. Laois in the Midlands of Ireland for most of his life. In 2008, James moved to England and studied in Oxford. James married his wife in 2012 and currently lives in Havant in Hampshire.

James had his first book, 365 Ways to Stop Sabotaging Your Life published in 2014.

James' second book, 365 Things People Believe That Aren't True went on to become a No. 1 Best Seller.

Books by James Egan

Fiction
Fairytale (A children's play)
Inherit the Earth

Non-fiction
1000 Facts about Film Directors
How to Psychologically Survive Cancer
1000 Facts about Space
1000 Facts about American Presidents
Adorable Animal Facts
1500 Facts about Video Games
500 Things People Believe That Aren't True
1000 Things People Believe That Aren't True
3000 Astounding Quotes
1000 Facts About Comic Book Characters
100 Classic Stories in 100 Pages
Words That Need to Exist in English
The Pocketbook of Phobias
500 Facts about Godzilla
365 Ways to Stop Sabotaging Your Life

3,000 Facts about the Greatest Movies Ever

by

James Egan

ISBN: 978-1-326-49287-8

Because of the dynamic nature of the Internet, any web addresses or links contain in this book may have changed since publication and may no longer be valid. The views expressed in this work are solely those of the author and do not necessarily reflect the views of the publisher, and the publisher herby disclaims any responsibility for them.

Any people depicted in stock imagery provided by Thinkstock are models, and such images are being used for illustrative purposes only.
Certain stock imagery © Thinkstock.

Lulu Publishing Services rev. date: 10/12/2015

Dedicated to

Mark,
the only guy who knows more about movies
than me

Content

8½
(1963)

1. During pre-production, Fellini forgot what the film was about. He then decided that the film would be about a director who forgot what he was directing.

2. This is the film that Fellini is proudest of.

3. Like all of his films, 8½ didn't have a finished script when Fellini started directing it.

4. Like most Italian films of the time, 8½ was shot without any sound. All recordings were dubbed in afterward.

5. While shooting, Fellini attached a note to his camera that said, "Remember, this is a comedy."

6. The original title was "The Beautiful Confusion."

7. Fellini considered Laurence Olivier for the lead.

8. Fellini cameos as a street magician.

9. This film was the inspiration for the musical, Nine.

10. At the time of shooting, Fellini had directed six films, two shorts and co-directed a film with Alberto Lattuda. As a result, he believed that he directed 8½ films. This is where he got the idea for the title.

12 Angry Men
(1957)

11.   This film is often used in business schools and workshops to illustrate team dynamics and conflict resolution techniques.

12.   This was Sidney Lumet's first directed film.

13.   The film was a flop.

14.   The actors had to rehearse in the same room for two weeks. They were ready to shoot much sooner but Lumet insisted that they needed to keep rehearsing. This left the actors frustrated as they said it would be impossible to shoot the film in the time left (twenty-one days.) However, this is exactly what Lumet wanted because he wanted the actors to look as frustrated as possible to add realism to their characters.

15.   Only three minutes of the film is not shot in the jury room.

16.   The jury room was 16 x 24 ft.

17.   The knife in the film is an Italian stiletto switchblade with a Filipino-style Kriss blade.

18.   Juror #7 looks at his watch twenty-eight times.

19.   No dialogue is spoken by a woman.

20.   The room appears smaller as the story progresses because Lumet uses longer focal lenses. This was done to make the characters seem more claustrophobic.

12 Years a Slave
(2014)

21. The director, Steve McQueen, wanted to write a story about a free black man who is forced to become a slave before he even knew the story of Solomon Northup existed.

22. Michael Fassbender passed out after the whipping scene.

23. This was Lupita Nyong'o's debut. She won an Oscar for Best Actress.

24. The hanging tree that Solomon looks at was actually used for lynching in its time. It is surrounded by the graves of murdered slaves.

25. The book that this story is based off sold terribly when it was released in 1853.

26. Brad Pitt was a producer

27. The film only took thirty-five days to shoot.

28. Chiwetel Eljiofor originally turned down the lead part.

29. This is the first film from a black director to win an Oscar for Best Picture.

30. Michael Fassbender had his makeup artist paint his moustache with alcohol so he would constantly taste it during his scenes.

The 400 Blows
(1959)

31. The title comes from the French phrase, "faire les quatre cents coups." It means, "to raise hell."

32. All of the actors who unsuccessfully auditioned for the lead were cast as the children in the classroom scenes.

33. This was directed by Francois Truffaut. It was his first film.

34. This is Ellen Page's favourite film.

35. The Finnish title is "400 Practical Jokes." The director said that this is a much more accurate title than "The 400 Blows."

36. All the lines had to be dubbed over by the actors.

37. The dialogue from the psychologist scene are ad-libbed.

38. Truffaut cameos as a man riding beside Antoine in the fair ride.

39. The film is dedicated to Andre Bazin. He was a film theorist.

40. Truffaut said that he was so happy with Jean-Pierre Leaud's audition for the lead of Antoine, that he edited some of it into the final cut.

2001: A Space Odyssey
(1968)

41.   The total footage shot was 200 times longer than the final cut of the film.

42.   The director, Stanley Kubrick, wanted to get an insurance policy to protect himself against losses in case aliens were discovered before film was released.

43.   Kubrick has tons of sand imported, washed and painted for the moon scenes.

44.   The film was nearly called "Voyage Beyond the Stars."

45.   There is no dialogue for the first twenty-five minutes of the film. In fact, eighty-eight minutes of the film is dialogue-free.

46.   This was the last film made about men on the moon before Neil Armstrong became the first man to walk on the moon.

47.   The villain is HAL 9000. Many television shows, films and cartoons parody HAL by saying, "Good morning, Dave." HAL never says this at any point.

48.   HAL was supposed to be called Athena.

49.   The earth-moving equipment seen on the moon weren't just props. They would actually work on the moon.

50.   The actors who play the apes in the beginning were mimes and dancers.

A Clockwork Orange
(1971)

51.　Alex and his droogs speak in a non-existent slang, which mixes English and Russian colloquialisms.

52.　Tim Curry and Jeremy Irons turned down the lead role of Alex.

53.　The spectacled body-builder near the end of the film is the Dave Prowse. He is more well-known for playing Darth Vader in Star Wars.

54.　Malcolm McDowell (who plays the lead role) had anaesthetic in his eyes for the torture scene.

55.　Malcolm McDowell had his corneas scratched and he was temporarily blinded when he was shooting the torture scene.

56.　The doctor in the torture scene was a real doctor.

57.　Stanley Kubrick would play table tennis with Malcolm McDowell in between scenes.

58.　Kubrick is known for drastically changing the source material when he turns books into films. However, this film resembles the original book more than anything other he has directed.

59.　McDowell was twenty-seven when he played the fifteen-year-old character, Alex.

60.　The snake scene was only in the film when Kubrick learned that McDowell was terrified of reptiles.

A Fistful of Dollars
(1964)

61.   It was supposed to be called "The Magnificent Stranger."

62.   Clint Eastwood had no idea that the film was a success because nobody told him that the title had changed. When he kept hearing about the success of "some film called A Fistful of Dollars," he was annoyed that no one was talking about his film.

63.   Clint Eastwood's famous squint became iconic due to this film. However, it wasn't his choice. He had to keep squinting due to the sun.

64.   Although this is considered the first Italian Western (or spaghetti western,) it is actually the twenty-fifth western produced in Italy. However, it is the first to receive a major international release.

65.   Although Clint's character is known as The Man With No Name, he is called Joe by the other characters.

66.   Clint had a contract for a film called Rawhide, which stipulated that he wasn't allowed to make an American film until Rawhide was released. As a result, Clint worked on this Italian film, which made his career take off and he became a part of arguably the greatest trilogy of all time.

67.   This is the first of the Dollars Trilogy (also known as The Man With No Name Trilogy.) The other films are For a Few Dollars More and The Good, the Bad and the Ugly. Only five actors are in all three films.

68.   It was released in 1964. However, it wasn't released in America until 1967.

69.   Most the crew and actors were Italian, German or Spanish which made it very difficult for everyone to communicate.

70.   Most of the crew knew nothing about the American West and Clint Eastwood had to educate most of the cast and crew about hats, coats, boots, shirts, etc.

A Streetcar Named Desire
(1951)

71.   Marlon Brando played the lead, Stanley Kowalski, in the play and won rave reviews for his machismo and charm. However, Brando hated that he was viewed as a sex-symbol because he based the character off the bullies who used to pick on him at school. When he got cast in the film, he bulked up even more and made his character appear dirty and sweaty. He was infuriated when Stanley Kowalski was considered one of the sexiest characters in film history.

72.   Nine actors who performed in the original play acted in this film.

73.   Sixty-eight changes had to be made from the Broadway play for the film to be considered acceptable by the censor board.

74.   This was the first film where an ordinary-sized actor bulked up for a part. Nowadays, it's common practice but at the time of this film, nobody had seen a physical transformation like Brando's. He was never known for being muscular until this film's release.

75.   Kowalski's apartment gets smaller throughout the film to highlight Blanche's paranoia.

76.   The studio wanted Robert Mitchum to play the lead role.

77.   Although the film has several locations, the play takes place entirely in Stanley's apartment.

78.   The play opened in 1947.

79.   Marlon Brando was the only actor in the film to be nominated for a Best Acting Oscar without winning.

80.   Vivian Leigh suffered from bipolar and would act the same way as Blanche in her later life.

The Adventures of Robin Hood
(1938)

81.   Anyone who was genuinely shot with an arrow was paid $150.

82.   Robin Hood died in the original script.

83.   The sound effect used when Robin fires an arrow has been used many times in the Star Wars films. The Star Wars sound operator, Ben Burtt, said it's his favourite sound effect ever.

84.   The film required eleven Technicolor cameras. At the time, these were the only Technicolor cameras in the world.

85.   The studio wanted James Cagney for the lead.

86.   Errol Flynn is the youngest actor to play Robin Hood. He was twenty-eight during this film.

87.   Robin Hood kills sixteen people.

88.   Orson Welles was offered the part of Friar Tuck.

89.   The film is based in 1191.

90.   Errol Flynn found his character dull.

The African Queen
(1951)

91. Humphrey Bogart claimed that he and the director drank so much alcohol throughout the shoot that "Whenever a fly bit Huston or me, it dropped dead."

92. Bogart's character was supposed to be Cockney. However, Bogart couldn't do the accent so it was changed to Canadian.

93. Walt Disney said this film inspired him to create the Jungle Cruise in Disneyland.

94. This was the first colour film that Katherine Hepburn acted in.

95. Bette Davis was considered for the lead.

96. The assistant director was Guy Hamilton. He is most famous for directing several Bond films, including Goldfinger.

97. Humphrey Bogart won his only Oscar for this film.

98. Real leeches were used for the leech scene.

99. Katherine Hepburn was so ill that a bucket was beside her in several shots as she would vomit between takes.

100. The cast and crew got sick from drinking water from the river. The only people who didn't become ill was John Huston and Humphrey Bogart because they only drank alcohol.

Akira
(1988)

101.   The film is based off a 2,500-page manga comic book.

102.   Since the comic is so gigantic, the film only deals with a very small portion of the story.

103.   Fifty colours were used for Akira that had never been used for an animated film.

104.   The main character is called Kanaeda. In the Japanese version, his name is pronounced "Canada." It's pronounced "Ka-nay-da" in the English dub because Western viewers would find it silly if the main character's name sounded the same as the country, Canada.

105.   Kanye West is a huge fan of Akira.

106.   It took eight years to write the Akira comic.

107.   The comic was so successful, that it was translated into English by Marvel Comics. This is one of the first times in history that a non-English comic series was completely translated into English.

108.   This was directed by Katsuhiro Otomo. He was the writer of the original comic.

109.   The Wachowski brothers said this film was the biggest influence for their film, The Matrix. When the film was re-released in 2001, it's tagline was, "No Akira, No Matrix."

110. The film contains 2,212 shots and 160,000 single pictures (which is three times more than an average animated film.)

Alien
(1979)

111.   Sigourney Weaver plays the part of Ripley. When she auditioned, she had no idea that the part was written for a man.

112.   The film was supposed to be called "Starbeast."

113.   The trailer is often considered the greatest film trailer ever.

114.   In the famous chest-bursting scene, none of the actors had a clue what was going to happen. Their terrified reactions are genuine.

115.   The story was pitched as "Jaws in space."

116.   No one was interested in funding the film until studios saw the success of Star Wars.

117.   The Xenomorph alien was inspired by Swiss artist, H.R. Giger.

118.   When 20th Century Fox saw the director's storyboards, they were so impressed, that they doubled the budget.

119.   When the director, Ridley Scott, shot exterior shots of the Nostromo ship, he was annoyed that the ship looked too small when the astronauts walked by the set. He decided to shoot the scene again with his two sons in much smaller astronaut suits to make the ship look gigantic. His idea worked.

120.   In the poster and trailer, the Xenomorph egg is actually a hen's egg.

Aliens
(1986)

121.   The knife trick scene wasn't in the script. The actor who plays Bishop, Lance Henriksen, decided to add it in at the last minute. He didn't discuss what he was going to do to the other actor, Bill Paxton, so his terrified screams are real.

122.   Sigourney Weaver was nominated for an Oscar for Best Actress. This was the first time a woman was ever nominated for Best Actress Oscar in an action film.

123.   A lot of film have an inaccurate countdown timer (e.g. a ten-minute timer might last five or twenty minutes.) However, the fifteen-minute countdown in this film is exactly fifteen minutes.

124.   The screams the aliens make are from baboons.

125.   Al Matthews is a black actor who plays a marine sergeant in the film. In reality, he was the first black Marine to be promoted to the rank of sergeant during Vietnam.

126.   At the time, the Alien Queen had the most puppeteers in film history. It took sixteen puppeteers to operate the Queen.

127.   Many of the crew were hostile to the director, James Cameron, as they were certain that he didn't know what he was doing with the film. This was before Cameron's film, The Terminator, was released so Cameron was not yet known as a visionary director.

    Cameron was even fired at one point. However, several of the crew and cast threatened to leave if he was fired. The whole issue was resolved.

This was the fourth time Cameron has been fired from a film. He was fired twice as the art director of the 1980 B-movie, Battle Beyond the Stars, and he was fired after a week of directing Piranha Part 2: The Spawning.

128.   Four actors appear in this film as well as the Terminator films. In The Terminator, Michael Biehn played Kyle Reese, Lance Henriksen played a cop and Bill Paxton played a punk. Jenette Goldstein played John Connor's foster mother in Terminator 2.

129.   Paul Reiser's sister found his character, Burke, so evil, that she punched him at the film's premiere.

130.   Carrie Henn plays the child, Newt. This is the only film she ever did.

All About Eve
(1950)

131.   This was the first of only two films ever to receive fourteen Oscar nominations, including Best Picture.

132.   This marked the first time where two actresses from the same film were Oscar nominated for Best Actress.

133.   This film has the record for the most female Oscar nominations for acting.

134.   Three of the actors committed suicide – Marilyn Monroe, George Sanders and Barbara Bates.

135.   Bette Davis filmed all of her scenes in sixteen days.

136.   Marilyn Monroe made filming a nightmare due to her inexperience and insecurities about working with established actors.

137.   Marilyn Monroe had to work with George Sanders. Sanders was married to Zsa Zsa Gabor, who was jealous that he was working with the beautiful Marilyn Monroe. She even showed up on set several times to make sure her husband wasn't cheating on her.

138.   Bette Davis said that this film saved her career. She said it, "resurrected me from the dead."

139.   It was originally supposed to be called "Best Performance."

140.   Ronald Reagan and Nancy Reagan were considered for the main roles.

All Quiet on the Western Front
(1930)

141.   Germany banned the film for making Germans look like cowards.

142.   Poland banned the film for being "pro-German."

143.   Before it was banned in Germany, Nazis would burst into cinemas that were showing the film with stink bombs and rats.

144.   Although it was banned in Germany, many Germans took a train or bus to Switzerland, France or the Netherlands to see it.

145.   It wasn't released in Germany until 1956.

146.   The film was banned in Italy until 1956.

147.   2,000 extras were used for the film.

148.   George Cukor (who would eventually direct My Fair Lady and A Star is Born) worked on the film as a dialogue coach.

149.   Fred Zinneman was another future director who worked on the film. (He was the director of Oklahoma!, From Here to Eternity and High Noon.) He plays an ambulance driver in the film. He was fired after two days.

150.   The film was extremely gory for its time. This is because the Production Code (the Censor Board) wasn't formed until 1934.

Amadeus
(1984)

151.   Although the film is considered a classic, all of the actors struggled to get work after. Even the lead actor's biggest role besides this one was the voice of Quasimodo in The Hunchback of Notre Dame.

152.   All of the musical keys struck on the pianos throughout the film are struck perfectly according to music experts analysing the film.

153.   Although this film is about the life of Mozart, he was never called Amadeus. His full name was Johannes Chrysostomus Wolfgangus Theophilus Mozart. Some of his friends called him Amade, but never Amadeus.

154.   The boy that Mozart smiles at in the party scene is Beethoven.

155.   Only four sets were built for the film.

156.   Mozart laugh is so odd in the film, it has become iconic. There is no evidence that Mozart laughed like this.

157.   Mark Hamill and Tim Curry played Mozart in the Amadeus play. They both auditioned for the part in the film but the role went to Tom Hulce.

158.   In order for Tom Hulce to prepare for the epic mood swings of Mozart, he studied temperamental tennis player, John McEnroe.

159.   When Mozart is dictating to Salieri what to write down, Tom Hulce intentionally kept giving

contradictory instructions so Salieri's confused reaction would look more genuine.

160.   The whole film was shot in natural light.

American Beauty
(1999)

161. When Lester throws the asparagus, he was supposed to throw it to the floor. The reaction of the other actors is genuine.

162. Lester Burnham's name is an anagram for "Humbert learns." This is a reference to the Vladimir Nabokov's book, Lolita, about a man who falls in love with a teenager.

163. Terry Gilliam was supposed to be the director.

164. Jeff Daniels auditioned for Lester..

165. Near the beginning of the film, Lester complains that he's missing a James Bond marathon. The director, Sam Mendes, went on to direct the Bond films, Skyfall and SPECTRE.

166. Kevin Spacey improvised everything he did in the car when he sang "American Woman."

167. The colour red is used over the colour white throughout the film e.g. roses in a white bath tub, blood on a white shirt, red car in front of a white door, etc.

168. It was Steven Spielberg's idea to have Sam Mendes direct this film.

169. In the original script, Lester's daughter Jane was sent to jail for murder.

170. A spin off television series was considered that would take place twenty years after the events of this film.

American History X
(1998)

171.   The director, Tony Kaye, did everything in his power to destroy the film. He was so unreasonable, that he was locked out of the editing room while the film's lead, Edward Norton, tried to save it.

    Not only that, but he bought forty full page ads in Variety and Hollywood Report criticizing the producers and accused them of stealing his film.

    But he didn't stop there. He even brought a rabbi, a priest and a Tibetan Buddhist monk with him to a meeting with the producers so that he could cut the film the way he wanted.

    Despite Kaye's lack of belief in the film, it received universal praise.

    Nevertheless, he had his name removed from the film.

172.   Tony Kaye got so frustrated during editing that he punched a wall and broke his hand.

173.   Joaquin Phoenix turned down the lead role.

174.   Kaye said he would only have his name credited for the film if he could be called Humpty Dumpty. When the studio said no (obviously,) Kaye strongly considered changing his name legally to Humpty Dumpty.

175.   Edward Norton turned down Saving Private Ryan to do this film.

176.   Norton gained 30lbs of muscle for the lead role.

177.   Marlon Brando was considered for a role.

178. Norton's character is based off a real skin-head called Frank Meeink.

179. The film was delayed by nearly a year due to Tony Kaye's interference.

180. Tony Kaye threatened to sue the studio for $275 million. It is unknown if he received any compensation.

Amorres Perros
(2000)

181.　The film can be translated as, "Love's a Bitch."

182.　This was shot in one of the most dangerous areas of Mexico City.

183.　The film received many complaints for the dog fight scenes.

184.　At the beginning, it emphasises that no animals were hurt while making this film. The reason this had to be said at the beginning was because many viewers couldn't believe that the dogs in the film weren't hurt or killed.

185.　All of the scenes where dogs are dying or dead were achieved by giving the dogs mild sedatives.

186.　The dogfights look vicious because they are edited so well. In reality, the dogs were simply playing.

187.　All of the dog scenes were supervised by the MSPCA.

188.　The bus driver is played by Gael Garcia Bernal's father.

189.　Nine cameras had to be used simultaneously to shoot the car crash scene.

190.　The film crew was robbed by street gangs several times throughout the shoot.

Anatomy of a Murder
(1959)

191.   This was the first film that George C. Scott was Oscar nominated for.

192.   The film was supposed to have many flashbacks but the director hated using them so they were not included.

193.   Spencer Tracey was offered the role of the judge.

194.   Gregory Peck was considered for the lead.

195.   Premiere voted this film as having the greatest movie poster ever.

196.   This film was originally banned in Chicago.

197.   This was the last film James Stewart was Oscar nominated for.

198.   James Stewart's father took out an ad in the newspaper telling people not to see this film, even though his son played the lead role.

199.   This film was incredibly controversial for its time due to using the words "contraceptive," "slut," "panties" and many others.

200.   The film was cut, scored and previewed one month after it wrapped.

Annie Hall
(1977)

201. The original title was "Anhedonia."

202. There was one scene that turned out so bad, Woody Allen threw it in the river.

203. Woody Allen's famous scene where he sneezes into a batch of cocaine wasn't intentional. It was a genuine sneeze.

204. The Truman Capote lookalike is actually Truman Capote.

205. This is Woody Allen's most successful film by far.

206. Woody Allen doesn't like this film.

207. Diane Keaton plays Annie Hall. Her real name is Diane Hall. Her nickname is Annie.

208. It is the second-shortest film to win the Oscar for Best Picture.

209. Annie Hall's iconic clothes are actually Diane Keaton's.

210. The film was originally supposed to be a period comedy in Victorian London.

Apocalypse Now
(1979)

211.   Marlon Brando was supposed to look muscular for his character, Kurtz. The director, Francis Ford Coppola, was infuriated to see that Brando weighed 300lbs. His scenes were shot in the dark to hide his size.

212.   Brando was told to read Heart of Darkness before he started filming. Not only did Brando refused to read the book but he didn't learn his lines and he turned the script into a hat so he wouldn't get sunburnt.

213.   While Brando was saying his lines in one scene, he started choking and then shouted, "I swallowed a bug!" You can see the clip on YouTube.

214.   The film took three years to edit. Everyone was convinced it would turn out to be a disaster. It is often hailed as the greatest war film ever made.

215.   The lead actor, Martin Sheen, had a heart attack during filming. His brother, Joe Estevez, had to stand-in for Martin while he recovered.

216.   Lawrence Fishburne was fourteen when production began. He only got the part because he lied about his age.

217.   Al Pacino was offered the lead role.

218.   The water buffalo at the end of the film was slaughtered for real.

219.   Marlon Brando improvised most of his dialogue.

220.   Coppola shot 200 hours of footage for the film.

The Artist
(2011)

221.   Jean Dujardin is the only French person to win a Best Actor Oscar.

222.   This is the first Best Picture winner that was produced by a non-English speaking country.

223.   There are no zoom shots in the film because zooms didn't exist during the silent era.

224.   Jack the dog was played by three Jack Russell Terriers.

225.   The film was shot in colour and then converted into black-and-white.

226.   This film received more awards than any French film in history.

227.   The final dance required five months of rehearsal.

228.   The final dance was performed in the same studio Gene Kelly and Debbie Reynolds danced for Singin' in the Rain.

229.   This is the first silent film to get a major cinema release since Silent Movie in 1976.

230.   This is the second silent film to ever win the Best Picture Oscar. The other film was Wings in 1927.

Back to the Future
(1985)

231.   Thomas F. Wilson plays the villain, Biff. He has been asked the same questions about the film so many times, that instead of answering them, he hands out cards that should answer every possible question about the films. It says things like -
"Michael J. Fox is nice.
Christopher Lloyd is shy.
Crispin Glover is unusual.
The third movie is my favourite.
The manure was made of peat moss, cork, dirt and a sticky food agent."

232.   Christopher Lloyd's character, Doc, seems hunched because he was so much taller than Michael J. Fox.

233.   The lead role was originally offered to Ralph Macchio, who is most famous for playing the lead role in The Karate Kid.

234.   Christopher Lloyd based Doc on Albert Einstein.

235.   John Lithgow was considered for the role of Doc.

236.   Crispin Glover based his performance as Old George off the lead character in the film, Eraserhead.

237.   This film is banned in China because the Chinese find time-travel disrespectful to history.

238.   Tim Robbins was considered for the role of Biff.

239.   The film was nearly called "Spaceman from Pluto."

240.   It was the most successful film of 1985.

Barry Lyndon
(1975)

241.   Shooting took 300 days over a two-year production, which got shutdown twice after the budget went way over.

242.   The director, Stanley Kubrick, did at least twenty takes for every shot but he would usually do up to fifty.

243.   Some shots took over a hundred takes.

244.   Some of the clothes in the film are not costumes. They are the actual clothes worn by the soldiers. They were bought in an antique shop.

245.   This is Lars von Trier's favourite film.

246.   Stanley Kubrick had to move the production from Ireland to England when he learned that his name was on the IRA hit list for directing a film featuring English soldiers in Ireland.

247.   Kubrick played classic music in-between shots to help the actors keep in the mood.

248.   Kubrick asked the actress, Marisa Berenson, to avoid the sun for months to maintain the pale complexion he desired for her character.

249.   Kubrick was so shy to the actresses that he would normally wouldn't speak to them at all. If he had to give them direction, he would write it on a note and hand it to them.

250.   Brian Blessed's scenes were cut.

Ben-Hur
(1959)

251.   This is the only religious Hollywood film that the Vatican approves of.

252.   During the chariot race, it is possible to see a red car in the background for a second.

253.   The chariot race was so complicated that no sound effects were used. All sound effects had to be inserted in afterward.

254.   Paul Newman was offered the part of Ben-Hur but he said he didn't have the legs to pull off a tunic.

255.   Although Charlton Heston already knew how to ride a two-horse chariot due to his work on The Ten Commandments, he had to learn how to handle a four-horse chariot for this film. He learned how to do it in four weeks.

256.   Three hundred sets, five years of research and over a year of construction were required for this film.

257.   Leslie Nielsen was nearly cast as the villain, Messala.

258.   There were forty versions of the script.

259.   This was the first film to win eleven Oscars.

260.   Over a million props were needed for this film. It took two years to locate all of the necessary props for the film before they shot a single scene.

The Best Years of Our Lives
(1946)

261.   The director, William Wyler, wanted to get someone who fought in World War II for the part of the wounded veteran, Homer Parish. Wyler discovered a former veteran called Harold Russell who lost his hands in a bombing. Wyler first saw Russell in an army training film called Diary of a Sergeant, which details the rehabilitation needed for wounded servicemen.

262.   Russell is the only person to win two Oscars for the same role. He won an Oscar for film and he also won an Honorary Oscar for inspiring veterans with his performance.

263.   Wyler wanted the buildings to look crummy so he built the sets slightly smaller than usual.

264.   The director was a major in the Army Air Force in World War II.

265.   This film is based off the novel, "Glory for Me."

266.   Although Russell won two Oscars for this film, he vanished into obscurity. He didn't make another film for thirty-two years and only has five acting credits to his name.

267.   Russell messed up his lines in the wedding scene. Wyler liked it because it showed how nervous a person would be on their wedding and, he kept the shot in.

268.   The character of Homer Parrish was supposed to only suffer mental side effects. But when the physically-impaired Harold Russell got the part, the script was rewritten to accommodate him.

269. Wyler despised the film's music, even though it won an Oscar.

270. A lot of the crew members were WWII veterans.

Bicycle Thieves
(1948)

271.   In one scene, Bruno nearly gets hit by two cars. This wasn't in the script. Two cars happened to pass by during that shot.

272.   None of the actors were professionals.

273.   The director, Vittorio De Sica, chose the two leads based on how they walked.

274.   Legendary film director, Sergio Leone, worked as an assistant on this film.

275.   Sergio Leone also cameos as a priest.

276.   De Sica said that Charlie Chaplin's films were the biggest inspiration for this film.

277.   The producers considered Cary Grant for the lead.

278.   The director considered Henry Fonda for the lead.

279.   The lead actor was Lamberto Maggiorani. Like his character, he struggled for work after he finished filming.

280.   The film was entirely shot in real locations.

The Big Lebowski
(1998)

281. The film has spawned a "religion" called Dudeism, where devotees embrace the philosophy of Jeff Bridges character, The Dude. It was set up in 2005 and has 130,000 "Dudeist Priests."

282. It is mentioned seventeen times that the Dude's rug was peed on. It is mentioned five times that it "really tied the room together."

283. The Dude was inspired by the film's promoter, Jeff Dowd.

284. The Dude never bowls at any point in the film.

285. John Turturro's character, Jesus, has a dance that was inspired by Muhammad Ali.

286. The coffee shop that The Dude and Walter meet in is the same coffee shop at the beginning of Reservoir Dogs.

287. Donny gets a strike with every bowl except the last one, minutes before he dies.

288. The Dude is in every scene.

289. The film is loosely based off Raymond Chandler's, The Big Sleep.

290. On The Dude's mantle piece is a picture of Richard Nixon bowling.

Black Swan
(2010)

291.   Natalie Portman trained as a ballerina dancer for a year for this role.

292.   Portman paid for her training out of her own money.

293.   The director, Darren Aronofsky, believes the film would've never been made if Portman wasn't on-board due to her unrealistic commitment to the project.

294.   There's a lot of subtle CGI (computer-generated images) throughout the film. In one scene, Nina's fingers seem overly long. This was done with CGI to make Nina seem like she was losing her grip on reality. When Nina comes off stage during the final show, several of the girls have Nina's face. Their faces can only be seen for a split-second and is very easy to miss.

295.   80% of the dance moves were performed by Portman. The rest were done by her double.

296.   Natalie Portman began ballet training before she was even cast.

297.   Portman married the film's choreographer, Benjamin Millepied.

298.   Portman hit her head in one scene and suffered a concussion.

299.   Meryl Streep was considered for Nina's mother.

300.   At the time of its release, it made more money than all of Aronofsky's previous films combined.

Blade Runner
(1982)

301. The film is supposed to take place in the same universe as Ridley Scott's other film, Alien.

302. Dustin Hoffman was considered for the lead.

303. The film was nearly called "Mechanismo."

304. There's a misconception that Harrison Ford was forced to do the film's narration against his will, which is why he sounds so bland.
    However, Ford has said that he was always on board with doing the narration but he is annoyed it didn't turn out as well as he hoped. He said that he did the best he could and he was frustrated that he sounded so bland.

305. Although Harrison Ford stresses that Deckard is human, the original script, the director, and the writer agree that he is a Replicant.

306. Ridley Scott believes that this is his best film.

307. This is one of the first films that had a director's cut.

308. The film is based off Philip K. Dick's book, Do Androids Dream of Electric Sheep?

309. Although Deckard is only called by his surname, his first name is Rick.

310. Contrary to popular belief, Rutger Hauer didn't improvise his final monologue. He only improvised the "like tears in the rain" line.

The Blues Brothers
(1980)

311.   This was Ray Charles film debut.

312.   John Belushi lost hundreds of pairs of sunglasses throughout the shoot. He became known as The Black Hole.

313.   The corrections officer is played by Frank Oz, who famously played Yoda in the Star Wars films.

314.   Dan Aykroyd plays the lead, Elwood. He saved his co-star, Carrie Fisher, from choking by performing the Heimlich manoeuvre. They got engaged soon after.

315.   The film was not released in many cinemas in the America South because there was too many African-Americans in it.

316.   The script was originally 324 pages long and was meant to be two films.

317.   Belushi's cocaine addiction was at its peak during the film. The director, John Landis, got so frustrated by Belushi's unpredictable behaviour that he stormed into Belushi's trailer and flushed his stash down the toilet.

318.   Little Richard was offered a part but he declined.

319.   Elwood never removes his glasses. Jake removes them once.

320.   103 cars were wrecked for the film. It was the world record at the time. It was beaten by The Matrix Reloaded when 300 cars were destroyed.

Bonnie & Clyde
(1967)

321. Warren Beatty plays the lead, Clyde Barrow. He was also the film's producer.

322. Beatty was never supposed to star in the film. When he was the producer, he wasn't even considered for a role until months later.

323. Roger Ebert was a film critic for six months when he saw this film. At the time, he said it was the best film he had seen.

324. Beret sales skyrocketed worldwide because Faye Dunaway wears one in the film.

325. Warner Brothers had no belief in the film and willingly allowed the star and producer, Warren Beatty to obtain 40% of the film's gross. The film made a profit of $50 million.

326. Warren Beatty wanted Bob Dylan to play Clyde.

327. Cher auditioned for the role of Bonnie.

328. Beatty wanted the film to be in black-and-white.

329. The tagline was simply, "We rob banks."

330. This was the film debut of Gene Wilder.

Braveheart
(1995)

331.   William Wallace was never called Braveheart. The nickname "Braveheart" was given to Robert the Bruce.

332.   Mel Gibson admitted that most of the film is fictitious and he was ten years too old to play Wallace.

333.   James Cosmo plays Campbell. His son, Hamish, is played by Brendan Gleeson. Although they are father and son, Cosmo is only seven years older than Gleeson.

334.   Many Scottish people were upset with Robert the Bruce's depiction as he is considered a Scottish hero.

335.   Some extras can be seen wearing sunglasses and watches.

336.   William Wallace famously says the line, "Every man dies, not every man really lives." Weirdly, this line was said by ANOTHER person called William Wallace. He was an American poet in the 19th century.

337.   Mel Gibson was investigated by an animal welfare organisation as they couldn't believe that this film could be made without the death of many horses. Mel showed them the videotaped footage to show that many of the "injured" horses were actually mechanical.

338.   Some of William Wallace's ancestors played extras in the film.

339.   Sean Connery was meant to play the villain, Longshanks.

340.   Most of the film was shot in Ireland.

The Breakfast Club
(1985)

341.   The script was written in two days.

342.   The scene where the characters have to explain why they are in detention was ad-libbed.

343.   Although Judd Nelson was playing a high-school teenager, he was twenty-six at the time of shooting.

344.   Nicholas Cage was considered for Bender.

345.   Judd Nelson visited a high school and convinced the kids there that he was one of the students. He did this to see if his character was convincing enough to fool other students.

346.   The film was nearly called "The Lunch Bunch."

347.   Rick Moranis was originally supposed to be in the film.

348.   Anthony Hall had a growth spurt during the production. Judd said that he was taller than Hall in the beginning but shorter than him by the end.

349.   Bender's fist-in-the-air at the end was ad-libbed.

350.   There were talks about having a sequel every ten years to see what the gang are up to. This never came to be as the director said he would never work with Judd Nelson again.

Bride of Frankenstein
(1935)

351.   Boris Karloff sweated 20lbs off by working in heavy makeup and thick clothing.

352.   The Bride's movements and hissing sounds are based off a swan.

353.   Elsa Lanchester plays the author of the Frankenstein novel, Mary Shelley, in the introduction. Lanchester also plays The Bride.

354.   Lanchester bandaged costume was so tight that she couldn't move her arms and had to be fed through a straw.

355.   Lanchester was only 5ft 4 so she had to wear seven inch lifts.

356.   Bela Lugosi was considered for Dr. Pretorius.

357.   Karloff was suffering severe arthritis throughout this film. The heavy demand of his role exasperated his illness.

358.   The Bride is in the film for less than five minutes.

359.   Elsa Lanchester isn't credited in the film.

360.   This is the first Frankenstein film where The Monster speaks. Boris Karloff was heavily against the idea.

The Bridge on the River Kwai
(1957)

361. Elephants were used to build the vast bridge. They would take breaks every four hours and would lie in the water.

362. The real bridge required 100,000 builders. 12,000 of them died during its construction.

363. Although many sources say that the bridge cost $250,000 to build, it was actually $52,000.

364. Construction on the bridge began before a single person was cast.

365. Spencer Tracy was nearly cast as the lead.

366. Alec Guinness was terribly insecure about his role and was worried it would come across as dull. However, the director and his own family believed that it was the best performance of his career.

367. There were no facilities to watch the film's dailies so the footage had to be flown to London and back.

368. The director, David Lean, nearly drowned at one point.

369. This is Will Smith's favourite film.

370. The crew had to deal with snakes throughout the entire shoot.

Butch Cassidy and the Sundance Kid
(1969)

371.   This film won more BAFTA awards than any other, with a grand total of nine.

372.   The film was supposed to star Steve McQueen and Warren Beatty.

373.   The real Butch Cassidy got the nickname "Butch" because he worked at a butcher shop. The Sundance Kid got his name because he shot a man in Sundance.

374.   Butch Cassidy's sister would come to the set and tell the cast stories about her outlaw brother.

375.   Butch and Sundance's gang were called The Wild Bunch. However, the film, The Wild Bunch came out at the same time so this film had to change the gang's name to The Hole in the Wall Gang to avoid confusion.

376.   Sam Elliott makes his debut as Card Player 2.

377.   The filmmakers wanted Bob Dylan to sing a song for the film but he refused.

378.   Paul Newman said he enjoyed shooting this film more than any other.

379.   Paul Newman said that the director, George Roy Hill, was the most efficient director he had ever worked with.

380.   Butch and Sundance were killed on November 7th 1908 in Bolivia. Nobody knows where their graves are.

Casablanca
(1942)

381.   The famous line, "Play it again, Sam" is never said once.

382.   Ingrid Berman was taller than Humphrey Bogart so he had to wear platform shoes in their scenes.

383.   The original title was "Everybody Comes to Rick's."

384.   The script was considered too dated, had too much dialogue and not enough sex.

385.   Bogart's wife kept arriving on set accusing him of having an affair with Bergman.

386.   Only one cast member had ever been to Casablanca.

387.   Many of the Nazis in the film were played by German Jews who escaped Nazi Germany.

388.   It was named the best screenplay ever by the Writers Guild of America.

389.   All of the shadows in the background were actually painted onto the set.

390.   The script was originally an unproduced play that was said to be universally dreadful.

Casino
(1995)

391.   Robert de Niro wears seventy costumes in the film.

392.   The budget for the costumes was a million dollars.

393.   De Niro's character, Ace, is a chain-smoker. To avoid continuity problems, De Niro held his cigarette at the same distance so it looks the same in every scene.

394.   The film's most brutal scene involves a man's head being crushed in a vise. The director, Martin Scorsese, said that he was certain the scene would be removed but it would allow him to keep the other gory scenes that were vital for the plot.
    Surprisingly, the vise scene was kept in.

395.   The gown that Sharon Stone wears weighed 45lbs. It was so heavy, that it gave Stone horrific back injuries.

396.   This is the last film that Scorsese and De Niro made together.

397.   The novel the story is based on wasn't even finished before filming began.

398.   Renowned critic, Gene Siskel, loathed this film.

399.   When Joe Pesci falls into the cornfield hole, he broke a rib. Weirdly, he broke the exact same rib when he was shooting Raging Bull.

400.   Madonna was cast as the lead female until Sharon Stone tracked down Scorsese and begged him to give her the part.

Casino Royale
(2006)

401.   The beginning chase scene took six weeks to shoot.

402.   Daniel Craig is the first actor to play Bond that is younger than the series itself.

403.   This is the first Bond film in twenty-seven years that is based off an Ian Fleming novel. That last one was Moonraker.

404.   Craig is the first actor to be nominated for a BAFTA for playing James Bond.

405.   This is the longest Bond film of the series. It is 144 minutes long.

406.   Although half of the film is the poker game, it only took nine days to shoot the poker scenes.

407.   Craig lost his two front teeth in the first fight scene. His dentist has to fly from London to Prague to replace them.

408.   Gerard Butler was considered for the lead role.

409.   The villain's name, Le Chiffre, is French for "The Cypher."

410.   In Romania, the villain's name is Smashed Eye.

411.   Scarlet Johansson was considered for the role of Vesper Lynd.

412.   Vesper appears for a second as the Queen of Spades in the intro.

413.   Tarantino was strongly considered as the director.

414.   Tarantino said if he directed it, he would've cast Samuel L. Jackson as Felix Leiter and Uma Thurman as Vesper.

415.   Daniel Craig has an iconic moment when he rises from the sea in his swimming trunks. This famous moment was created by accident. The reason why Craig suddenly rises is because he walked on a sand hump.

416.   Craig gained 20lbs of muscle for the film.

417.   The film's codename was "Change at Midnight."

418.   Le Chiffre suffers haemolacria, a condition that makes him weep blood. This is usually caused from a tumour in the brain.

419.   Although Clive Owen was the fan-favourite for Bond, he never auditioned, nor was he ever considered.

420.   This was the first Bond film that wasn't illegal to watch in China.

Cat on a Hot Tin Roof
(1958)

421.   Elizabeth Taylor started shooting the same day her husband was killed.

422.   This film is based off the Tennessee Williams play. The play has several homosexual references but all of them were removed from the film.

423.   Marilyn Monroe was considered for Maggie.

424.   Montgomery Clift turned down the role of Brick.

425.   James Dean was considered for the role of Brick.

426.   The film was originally going to be in black-and-white.

427.   The play won a Pulitzer Prize in 1955.

428.   Grace Kelly was interested in playing Maggie.

429.   Elvis Presley was interested in playing Brick.

430.   After Elizabeth Taylor learned that her husband died, she developed a crippling stutter for months. However, it vanished as soon as the director said, "Action!" and only returned when he said, "Cut!"

Chinatown
(1974)

431.   There's a scene where John Huston says, "Do you sleep with my daughter?" to Jack Nicholson's character. By a freakish coincidence, Nicholson just started a relationship with John's daughter, Angelica Huston.

432.   The screenplay is often taught in screen writing classes on how to write a perfect script.

433.   This is the last film that Roman Polanski made in America before he fled to Europe to avoid criminal charges.

434.   Jack Nicholson kept being late for shooting because he was watching sports on tv. The director put an end to it when he broke the tv with a mop.

435.   Roman Polanski cameos as the man who cut's Gittes nose.

436.   "Chinatown" is slang which means "being involved with something too big to understand."

437.   Jack Nicholson hates the ending.

438.   Roman Polanski created the disturbing ending to deal with the trauma he suffered after his own wife was murdered by Charles Manson's cult.

439.   The film was originally meant to have narration but it was cut as the director thought it would be better if the audience was trying to put the clues together at the same pace as the main character.

440.   The film has a lesser known sequel called The Two Jakes. It was directed by Jack Nicholson himself.

Citizen Kane
(1941)

441.   The film is famously based off newspaper mogul, William Randolph Hearst. Since Hearst controlled the newspapers, he destroyed the film's reputation and accused the director and actor, Orson Welles of being a Communist. The film was a flop.

442.   It was booed at the Oscars every time one of its nine nominations was announced.

443.   During filming, Welles was told that William Randolph Hearst arranged a naked woman to jump at Welles when he entered his hotel room and a photographer was waiting inside the room to take a picture. This would then be used to tarnish the film beyond repair. Welles slept elsewhere on the day he received this threat.

444.   The film begins with the title and doesn't mention the actors. This was unprecedented at the time but it is very common nowadays.

445.   Welles hated how rooms in films looked like sets, so he created many low shots in this film so the audience could see the ceiling of the rooms and they would believe the characters were in a house, rather than a set.

446.   Orson Welles starred, directed, wrote and produced the film when he was only twenty-five.

447.   When Kane gives his speech on the podium, the audience is actually a photograph.

448.   Welles said that they had to use more makeup and camera techniques to make him look young rather than when he was playing Kane as an old man.

449.   Although it is known as the greatest film of all time, at the time of this book's publication, it is ranked #65 in the top 250 greatest films on IMDB (Internet Movie Database.)

450.   The scene where Kane destroys Susan's room was done in one take.

City of God
(2002)

451. The director said that he would have never made the film if he knew how dangerous the area was.

452. It is often called "the Brazilian Goodfellas."

453. Leandro Firmino (who plays one of the main characters) was actually from the City of God.

454. Firmino only went to the audition to keep his friend company. He had no ambition to be an actor.

455. The scene where the gang start praying before the war was unscripted.

456. When Knockout Ned kills a person, he is congratulated by a small group. The first person to congratulate him is the mother of the real Knockout Ned.

457. When Buscape tells Marina that "he never took a hot bath," he didn't realise that the cameras were on.

458. All of the actors lived in slums.

459. None of the actors had acted before.

460. None of the film was actually shot in the City of God as it was too dangerous.

City Lights
(1931)

461.   This film has the world record for the most takes of a scene (The Shining inaccurately gets this reputation.) The scene where the Little Tramp buys a flower from the flower-girl took 342 takes.

462.   Winston Churchill visited the set.

463.   This was the first film Chaplin made during the sound era.

464.   This is Woody Allen's favourite film.

465.   Virginia Cherrill plays the blind girl. In reality, she was very near-sighted.

466.   Chaplin spotted Cherrill at a boxing match and cast her for the part immediately.

467.   This was the longest produced film of Chaplin. It took over three years to make.

468.   Chaplin shot the film for 180 days.

469.   Chaplin invited Albert Einstein and his wife to the premiere. Chaplin saw Einstein crying at the end of the film

470.   Chaplin believed that talkies (films with sound and dialogue) were a fad while he was making this film. He fell under a huge amount of pressure when he realised that talkies were replacing silent films.

471.   Charlie Chaplin said this was favourite of the Little Tramp stories.

472.   It was supposed to be set in Paris.

473.   Chaplin owned his own studio so he had total control over the film.

474.   He kept his cast and crew on standby for twenty-two months.

475.   The film cost $1.5 million, an enormous amount for the time.

476.   Chaplin put his own money forward for the film.

477.   Chaplin composed the film score for the first time for this film.

478.   In the middle of production, Chaplin made a short with Winston Churchill.

479.   Chaplin was worried that audience members might assume that the film had sound. To remind them that it would be a silent film, it was billed as "a comedy romance in pantomime written and directed by Charles Chaplin."

480.   This is Stanley Kubrick's favourite film.

The Conversation
(1974)

481. The film was originally supposed to be a horror.

482. In the film, Enemy of the State, Gene Hackman plays Lyle, a former NSA agent who uses surveillance to spy on people. The character is supposed to be an older version of his character in this film.

483. Harry Caul was supposed to be called Harry Call but his named was changed due to a typo.

484. This is the film the Hackman is proudest of.

485. Robert Duvall cameos as the director who hires Caul.

486. Hackman learned to play the saxophone for his character.

487. Coppola wrote this in 1966 but couldn't get funding for nearly eight years.

488. This is Francis Ford Coppola's favourite film.

489. Hackman said he wanted to grow a "pathetic-looking moustache" for his character.

490. Marlon Brando was considered for the lead.

Cool Hand Luke
(1967)

491. In the road-tarring scene, the actors genuinely tarred a mile of road.

492. The film has a famous scene where Paul Newman's character has to eat fifty eggs. Johnny Knoxville actually did this in his show, Jackass.

493. Paul Newman only ate eight eggs while filming the egg scene.

494. Jack Lemmon was supposed to play Luke.

495. Luke is seen as a saviour to the prisoners. After the egg scene, he lies out on the table in the shape of Jesus on a cross.

496. Jack Lemmon was a producer of the film.

497. Newman had to learn to play the banjo for the role of Luke.

498. Although Dennis Hopper is in the film, he doesn't have any dialogue.

499. Bette Davis turned down the part of Luke's mother.

500. Luke's prison number is 37. This is a Biblical reference to Luke 1:37, "For with God nothing shall be impossible."

Dancing with Wolves
(1990)

501.   Some actors had difficulty learning their lines in Sioux. Kevin Costner said he would fire anyone who couldn't.

502.   Marlon Brando was considered for the role of Maury.

503.   The dead deer that Costner pulls out of the river aren't props. They were deer that were killed on nearby highways.

504.   Kevin Costner did all of his own riding.

505.   Costner was worried that he might get into trouble for animal cruelty. To avoid this, an animatronic buffalo was built for the more violent scenes. It cost $250,000.

506.   The buffalo herd was made up of 3,500 animals.

507.   The scene where the buffalo charges at the Indian was accomplished by enticing the buffalo with a pile of Oreo cookies.

508.   Stands with A Fist is played by Kevin Costner's daughter, Annie.

509.   75% of the dialogue is in English.

510.   This is the most successful Western of all time. It made $184 million.

The Dark Knight
(2008)

511.   Steve Carell, Adrien Brody and Robin Williams wanted to play the Joker.

512.   The director, Christopher Nolan, said he never considered anyone for the Joker except Heath Ledger because "he is fearless."

513.   Heath Ledger was cast before there was a finished script.

514.   Heath Ledger said he would never do a superhero film shortly before being cast as the Joker.

515.   When James Gordon is promoted to commissioner, Heath Ledger's clapping was improvised.

516.   The money pile that Joker burns was calculated to be $6.328 billion dollars.

517.   Heath Ledger wrote a Joker journal in his hotel room over a six-week period.

518.   Christopher Nolan encouraged the cast and crew to watch Citizen Kane, King Kong, Stalag 17, Cat People, A Clockwork Orange, Cat People and Black Sunday. They probably had to watch Batman Begins too.

519.   Michael Caine was supposed to have a line when he meets the Joker but he forgot it because he had not seen Heath Ledger as the Joker until that moment and Heath freaked him out.

520.   Liev Schreiber was considered for Two-Face.

Das Boot
(1981)

521.   Although it was filmed in German, all of the actors could speak English. The actors dubbed themselves for the English dub.

522.   The film was shot in silence. All the dialogue and sounds were inserted in post production.

523.   The cast rarely ventured outside during shooting so they would look as pale as an actual submarine crew.

524.   Some distant shots of the submarine are of a small submarine model. The "people" in these shots are actually Ken and Barbie dolls.

525.   Four out of five of the main characters are never named.

526.   Rutger Hauer was offered the role of the Captain but he turned it down to do Blade Runner.

527.   The director's wife, Maria, decided who died in the film's conclusion.

528.   The film was nominated for six Oscars. At the time, this was the most Oscar nominations for a foreign film.

529.   The film was shot in sequence.

530.   Although the director could've removed sections of the walls to make shots easier, he decided not to in order to maintain the claustrophobia that submariners suffer.

The Deer Hunter
(1978)

531.   All of the slapping in the Russian roulette scenes was genuine.

532.   Robert De Niro said that the hospital visit scene was the most emotional scene of his career.

533.   Twenty-eight deaths related to Russian roulette occurred shortly after this film was released.

534.   Christopher Walken improvised spitting in De Niro's face in one scene.

535.   This was John Cazale's final film. Cazale only starred in the greatest films ever – The Godfather, The Godfather: Part II, The Conversation, Dog Day Afternoon and The Deer Hunter. Some actors say he has the best acting CV in the word (despite how small it is.)

536.   To prepare for the part, De Niro worked with steelworkers under the alias of Bob. No one recognised him.

537.   Meryl Streep improvised most of her lines.

538.   John Cazale was so ill, that they shot his scenes first. He died shortly after.

539.   De Niro said this was the most physically exhausting film he has ever done.

540.   Walken wanted to look gaunt and shrivelled so he ate nothing but bananas and rice for weeks.

The Departed
(2006)

541.   Frank Costello's part was much smaller before Jack Nicholson was cast.

542.   Mark Wahlberg was arrest over twenty times as a youth so his performance as a police officer is based off the cops who arrested him.

543.   The director, Martin Scorsese, claims that this was the first film he had directed that had a plot.

544.   Scorsese finished the film one week before its release.

545.   Brad Pitt and Tom Cruise were meant to play the lead characters.

546.   This film is a remake of Infernal Affairs. Scorsese didn't watch it until he finished this film.

547.   Alec Baldwin's part was supposed to be played by Mel Gibson.

548.   Nicholson improvised most of his scenes.

549.   The rat at the end is digital.

550.   The title doesn't appear for eighteen minutes.

Dial M for Murder
(1954)

551.   Grace Kelly has bright clothes at the beginning of the title. They get darker as the story progresses.

552.   The director, Alfred Hitchcock, wanted Cary Grant to play the villain.

553.   Hitchcock cameos thirteen minutes into the film in a photograph.

554.   Hitchcock had to do the scissors stabbing scene several times until the scissors "gleamed." He said "a murder without gleaming scissors is like asparagus without the hollandaise sauce – tasteless."

555.   Many Hitchcock films have a MacGuffin. A MacGuffin is a plot device that motivates a character and progresses the story but it has very little relevance to the story itself. In this film, the MacGuffin is the latch key.

556.   The film was shot in 3-D, much to Hitchcock's dissatisfaction.

557.   The film was shot in thirty-six days.

558.   This is one of three films that Grace Kelly did with Hitchcock. She also starred in to Catch a Thief and Rear Window.

559.   A remake called A Perfect Murder was released in 1998.

560.   Hitchcock lost 20lbs while making this film.

Die Hard
(1988)

561. This was Alan Rickman's film debut.

562. The German that Gruber says into the phone is not real German.

563. The script was nearly turned into Commando 2, starring Arnold Schwarzenegger.

564. For Gruber's final scene, Rickman was told he would be dropped five feet out of the building, while being attached to a harness. However, he was dropped twenty-one feet. The terrified expression on his face is genuine as he thought he was about to plummet to his death.

565. Hans Gruber's famous fall was filmed at 300 frames per second.

566. Rickman jumped almost every time a gun fired. You can still see him wince when he shoots Takagi.

567. Rickman was certain he was going to be fired throughout the shoot.

568. Rickman nearly broke his leg on the first week. In most of the scenes where he is talking to John McClane, Rickman is wearing a leg brace underneath his trousers.

569. When Bruce Willis runs through the broken glass, he is actually wearing rubber shoes.

570. Bruce Willis was shooting the television series, Moonlighting, at the same time as this film.

571.   Although the Germans mock John McClane for being the "all-American hero," Bruce Willis was actually born to a German mother in Germany.

572.   This is based off the book, Nothing Lasts Forever, which is loosely based off a true story.

573.   Clint Eastwood originally had the rights to the novel, Nothing Lasts Forever. He wanted to produce and star in the film but he never found a convenient time to do it.

574.   The studio wanted Robert De Niro to play John McClane.

575.   The building that the film takes place in is the headquarters of 20th Century Fox.

576.   Sam Neill was meant to play the villain.

577.   In Hungary, the film is called "Give Your Life Expensive." Die Hard 2 is called "Your Life is More Expensive." Die Hard with a Vengeance is called "The Life is Always Expensive."

578.   The blanks from the guns were so loud that Bruce Willis suffers from hearing loss to this day.

579.   Alan Rickman was cast as the villain after the director and producer saw him in the play, Dangerous Liaisons. He played Vicomte de Valmont.

580.   Many of the explosions were real including the explosions that can be seen in the exterior shots of the building.

Django Unchained
(2012)

581. When Leonardo DiCaprio's character, Calvin Candie, smashes the palm of his hand onto the table, it started to bleed. DiCaprio acted like a professional and carried on with the scene. This means that the blood he smears into Broomhilda's face is his actual blood.

582. DiCaprio stopped a scene because he felt uncomfortable saying racial slurs to a room full of black people. Samuel L. Jackson then said, "This is just another Tuesday for us."

583. Jamie Foxx's horse in the film is his own horse, Cheetah.

584. Christoph Waltz fell off his horse at one point and broke his pelvis.

585. This is the first film in sixteen years where Leonardo DiCaprio didn't get top billing.

586. The poker players at the end of the film are using slave ears as currency.

587. Broomhilda's surname is Von Shaft. According to the director, Quentin Tarantino, Broomhilda is supposed to be the great-great-great-grandparent of John Shaft from the Shaft series.

588. Django means "I wake."

589. Will Smith was offered the lead role but he declined.

590. While Tarantino was shooting, he rented a cinema to show his own personal collection of Western film.

591. The film was shot in 130 days. That means that Django Unchained has the longest shooting schedule of any of Tarantino's films.

592. There is a secret scene after the film ends.

593. This is the sixth film that Samuel L. Jackson has done with Tarantino.

594. Jamie Foxx and Kerry Washington portray a married couple in the film. They also played a married couple in the film, Ray.

595. Tarantino doesn't consider this film as a Western.

596. This is the most expensive film that Tarantino has ever made.

597. Christoph Waltz won an Oscar for Best Supporting Actor in his role as King Schultz. Since he is in the film for 1 hour, 16 minutes and 17 seconds, this is the longest performance to win an Oscar for Best Supporting Actor.

598. Tarantino cameos as a mining employee. He had to do an Australian accent because he couldn't do a Southern accent.

599. Tarantino only cameoed because the actor that was supposed to play his part didn't show up.

600. Tarantino also cameos as a baghead in the Regulator scene.

Dog Day Afternoon
(1975)

601.   Al Pacino's character, Sonny, is based off the bank robber, John Wojtowicz. John watched The Godfather the day he committed the robbery this film is based off. Al Pacino is the lead in The Godfather.

602.   John Wojtowicz received a twenty-year sentence for his crimes scene in the film. He only served five years.

603.   Pacino originally turned down the role, worried that it would conflict with filming The Godfather: Part II.

604.   This film has the most accurate hostage negotiation scene in film history. It is so accurate, that this film is used to teach negotiators how to deal with a hostage situation.

605.   Most of the dialogue is improvised. Pacino's famous shouting of "Attica! Attica!" was ad-libbed.

606.   To make his character look and act more erratic, Pacino barely ate or slept and only had cold showers.

607.   The original title was "Boys in the Bank."

608.   Pacino heard of the robbery that the film is based off while it was happening.

609.   Even though the film revolves around a bank robbery, only two shots are fired.

610.   John Wojtowicz was paid $7,500 and 1% of the film's profit.

Donnie Darko
(2001)

611.   This was Seth Rogen's film debut.

612.   Mark Wahlberg was interested in playing Donnie but he said he would only do it if he could have a lisp.

613.   Vince Vaughn turned down the lead.

614.   Jason Schwartzman was offered the part of Donnie but he dropped out because he was committed to another project.

615.   Many of the characters have the same letter for both of their names – Donnie Darko, Cherita Chen, Frankie Feedler, Daye Dennis, Sean Smith, Joanie James, etc.

616.   The actors who play Donnie Darko and Elizabeth Darko are siblings in real life.

617.   Mara Wilson was considered for Donnie's sister.

618.   Tim Robbins nearly played Donnie's father.

619.   The film is based off a 2007 play.

620.   Frank gets shot in the eye. When we see Frank after time has reset, he is wiping the eye that he was shot in.

Downfall
(2004)

621.   Bruno Ganz, who portrayed Hitler, studied Parkinson's disease patients at a hospital to prepare for this role.

622.   Bruno Ganz is Swiss.

623.   Ganz developed his accent for the role with the help of an Austrian man who lived in the same town as Hitler.

624.   At the premiere, most of the audience broke down crying and stayed until the end of the credits.

625.   Thirty-seven characters in the film are based off real people. Rochus Misch was the only one of them that was still alive when the film was released. He died in 2013 at the age of ninety-six.

626.   Ganz didn't want the role at first, believing it almost impossible to play Hitler without turning him into a clichéd villain.

627.   Hitler's former secretary, Traudl Junge, was in hospital when the film was released. When she was told that the film was a major success, she said, "My lifework is accomplished. Now I can let go." She died hours later.

628.   Most of the city scenes were shot in St. Petersburg, Russia.

629.   Many of Hitler's lines are identical to what he said in the same circumstances.

630. There is only one recording of Hitler in private. Ganz had to study the recording to hear Hitler's actual voice rather than his theatrical performance that is often seen in his speeches.

Dr. Strangelove or:
How I Learned to Stop Worrying and Love the Bomb
(1964)

631.   George C. Scott was so frustrated by Stanlet Kubrick demanding multiple takes that he overacted his last scene. Scott was even more enraged when this was the take that Kubrick used for the final cut.

632.   The glove that Peter Sellers wears for Dr. Strangelove wasn't a prop. It was Sellers' actual glove.

633.   The film was supposed to end with a custard pie fight. This is why there is so much food on the War Room table.

634.   Kubrick read fifty books about nuclear war to prepare for this film.

635.   George C. Scott trips in one scene. Kubrick left it in the film because he though Scott was acting and he didn't realise that he genuinely tripped.

636.   Sellers hated multiple takes and he believed he got worse after every take. Ironically, Kubrick and the rest of the cast and crew believed he got better after each take.

637.   Dr. Strangelove's suffers from agonistic apraxia which forces his hand to move against his will. Nowadays, this condition is more commonly known as Dr. Strangelove Syndrome.

638.   This was the first film where an actor (Peter Sellers) was nominated for a single Oscar for playing three different characters.

639.   The famous "Mein Fuhrer! I can walk!" line was improvised by Peter Sellers.

640.   In one version of the script, aliens observed all of the bombs going off.

641.   This was the film debut of James Earl Jones.

642.   James Earl Jones was cast after Kubrick saw him in a production of The Merchant of Venice. George C. Scott was in the same production.

643.   Kubrick was known for being a very serious man. However, he would laugh so much at Peter Sellers that he would be brought to tears.

644.   This is Gene Siskel's favourite film.

645.   Sellers was meant to play a fourth character with a Texan accent. It was scrapped because Sellers couldn't do the accent.

646.   It has the longest title for a Best Picture nominee or winner.

647.   Sterling Hayden plays a paranoiac who is scared of Communists. In reality, he was a part of the American Communist Party.

648.   The film was supposed to be released on the day that JFK was shot. It was delayed by two months.

649.   This was the final black-and-white film released by Kubrick.

650.   It was supposed to be called "The Edge of Doom."

East of Eden
(1955)

651.   The film is based off the John Steinbeck novel of the same name. However, the film doesn't cover much of the first half of the novel.

652.   Marlon Brando was considered for the role of Cal.

653.   Montgomery Clift was considered for the role of Aaron.

654.   James Dean screen-tested with Paul Newman.

655.   This is Ryan Gosling's favourite film.

656.   James Dean was actually drunk for the rooftop scene.

657.   Nicholas Cage said he wanted to be an actor because he "wanted to be James Dean."

658.   James Dean didn't attend the premier.

659.   The film was shot in ten weeks.

660.   When John Steinbeck met James Dean, he said, "Jesus Christ, he IS Cal!"

Ed Wood
(1994)

661. Ed Wood's wife, Kathy, arrived on the set to meet Johnny Depp, who was portraying her husband. As soon as she saw him, she said, "That's my Eddie."

662. Bela Lugosi's son, Bela Lugosi Jr., was hesitant to see the film, worried that his father would be portrayed as a joke. However, he was wowed by Martin Landau's performance as Lugosi and the two became friends.

663. Bela Lugosi Jr. said that his father's never used vulgar language like the way the film depicts.

664. Martin Landau won an Oscar for playing Dracula actor, Bela Lugosi. This was the first time an actor won an Oscar for portraying another actor.

665. Tim Burton said that he was fascinated by the Ed Wood because he thought Ed's relationship with Lugosi was similar to Burton's relationship to actor, Vincent Price.

666. This was the first R rated film directed by Tim Burton.

667. In the film, Lugosi keeps mocking Boris Karloff. In real life, they were friends and worked together several times.

668. In the film, Lugosi laments that he had the chance to play Frankenstein's Monster. In reality, he did play the role. He replaced Boris Karloff and played the Monster in Frankenstein Meets the Wolf Man.

669.   The opening monologue is a parody of Criswell's monologue at the beginning of Plan 9 From Outer Space.

670.   This film cost more than all of Ed Wood's films combined.

Edward Scissorhands
(1990)

671. Nobody wanted Johnny Depp to play Edward except for the director, Tim Burton.

672. Depp lost 25lbs for the part.

673. Burton conceived the story when he was a teenager.

674. The Inventor was written for Vincent Price.

675. This was Vincent Price's final film. His part was meant to be larger but he was near death when he started filming. The last scene he ever shot was his death scene.

676. Winona Ryder was supposed to be in The Godfather: Part III but she dropped out for this film.

677. Gary Oldman was offered the part of Edward but he turned it down.

678. The film was supposed to be a musical.

679. Tim Burton says he is proudest of this film.

680. Burton said that the film has the best musical score of all of his films.

681. Michael Jackson wanted to play Edward.

682. Drew Barrymore was considered for the part of Kim.

683. Crispin Glover was considered for the villain, Jim.

684.	Edward only speaks 169 words in the film.

685.	Johnny Depp's debut film was A Nightmare on Elm Street where he was killed by a killer with blades on his fingers.

686.	Depp was extremely hot in his leather suit. Nevertheless, he refused to do anything to cool him down as he was worried it would interfere with his character. In the scene where he runs back to the castle, Depp collapsed from heat exhaustion.

687.	The town is based off Tim Burton's hometown of Burbank in California.

688.	The windows in the houses are intentionally small to make them seem more "paranoid."

689.	Caroline Thompson plays Peg, the woman who finds Edward. She based her character off her mother.

690.	Originally, Caroline Thompson thought the film had the stupidest story she had ever heard.

The Elephant Man
(1980)

691.   The Elephant Man is known as John Merrick in the film. In reality, he was called Joseph Merrick.

692.   It took eight hours to apply the Elephant Man makeup to John Hurt and it took two hours to remove it. He would arrive on set at 5am and shoot from 12pm to 10pm.

693.   John Hurt had to work alternate days because he couldn't take the weight of the mask daily.

694.   John Hurt's makeup was designed directly from the casts made of Merrick's skull.

695.   Although Merrick's circus owner seems like a tyrant, in reality, he was very kind to Merrick.

696.   David Lynch was fixing roof tiles when he got the job as the film's director.

697.   When Anthony Hopkins character, Frederick Treves, sees the Elephant Man for the first time, a single tear falls out of Hopkins' eye. Hopkins said he thought of the time his father was ill during this scene.

698.   The makeup was so detailed for this film that the Oscars created the Best Makeup category the following year.

699.   Merrick speaks much clearer in the film than he did in real life. In reality, his doctor was his interpreter as nobody else could understand him.

700.   After Hurt's first day wearing the makeup, he said to his wife, "I think they finally managed to make me hate acting."

701.   At the start of the film, Merrick's mother seems to be attacked by an elephant. Although this never happened, this story was told in Merrick's circus.

702.   Terence Malick declined the director's chair.

703.   Merrick isn't seen for thirteen minutes. He doesn't speak until forty minutes into the film.

704.   Hurt was supposed to wear a body suit but the director realised it would be physically impractical.

705.   Lynch got the job thanks to Mel Brooks, who was the film's executive producer.

706.   Alderman tries to close down the freak show at the beginning of the film. He is played by the great-nephew of Merrick's doctor.

707.   Lynch cameos as one of the mob chasing Merrick in the train station.

708.   Despite what many people believe, Merrick didn't suffer from elephantiasis. He probably suffered from Proteus Syndrome, neurofibromatosis and an unnamed bone deformity.

709.   Joseph Merrick died when he was twenty-seven.

710.   The Orc leader, Gothmog, in Lord of the Rings: Return of the King, was inspired by The Elephant Man. Weirdly, John Hurt played Aragorn in the 1978 film, The Lord of the Rings.

Eternal Sunshine of the Spotless Mind
(2004)

711.   Most of the astounding effects were created with editing, lighting and camera tricks. Computer effects were only used when nothing else was possible.

712.   The title comes from an Alexander Pope poem.

713.   The memory-erasing company is called Lacuna. A lacuna is a fluid-filled hole in the brain after a stroke or seizure.

714.   A fully functional website was created for Lacuna called www.lacunainc.com

715.   Kate Winslet said this film has her favourite performance.

716.   The title doesn't appear for eighteen minutes.

717.   When Mark Ruffalo's character, Stan, scares Kirsten Dunst, he appeared from a different spot on each take so her reaction seemed genuine.

718.   The scene where Joel and Clementine watch the circus wasn't intentional. The circus happened to be going on during shooting.

719.   Kate Winslet punched Jim Carrey for real during the train scene. Carrey wasn't expecting it.

720.   When Joel is in his head and he visits his session of the erasing process, no special effects were used to show two Jim Carreys. Carrey just moved really fast and swapped his clothes back and forth.

Fanny and Alexander
(1982)

721.   The first draft was 1,000 pages.

722.   The film was over three hours. However, Ingmar Bergman made a 5 hr 48 min version of the film. This version was his favourite.

723.   At the time, this was the biggest and most expensive Swedish film ever made. It cost $6 million and had 1,200 actors.

724.   Bergman didn't tell the lead actor, Bertil Guve, what the film was about. This was to stop the actor from being too self-conscious of his performance.

725.   Bergman suffered tremendous hypochondria throughout filming and he was convinced that he had stomach and testicular cancer.

726.   Bergman stated in his autobiography that Charles Dickens was the biggest inspiration for the film.

727.   The film was shot in chronological order.

728.   A young Peter Stormare plays the man helping Isak with the trunk. Stormare is famous for playing the Russian in Armageddon and Satan in Constantine.

729.   Jan Malmsjo was shooting the film and doing a play at the same time. He collapsed once due to exhaustion.

730.   This was the last theatrical film directed by Bergman.

Fargo
(1996)

731. William H. Macy stutters so much in the film, that many people assumed that he was ad-libbing. He wasn't. Every stutter and stumble he uttered was written in the script.

732. Frances McDormand had a pregnancy pillow filled with birdseed to make her look pregnant.

733. The only part of this film that's "based off a true story" is there was a man who was killed by another person by a woodchipper. The rest of the story is entirely fictional.

734. Since the film wasn't based on a true story as it claims to be, William H. Macy was worried that the directors would be sued.

735. Although Frances McDormand is the lead, she doesn't appear for thirty-three minutes.

736. A television show of Fargo was supposed to be released in 1997.

737. This is one of six film that Steve Buscemi has worked on with the Coen brothers.

738. When she was asked how she got the part in Fargo, Frances McDormand said, "The fact that I'm sleeping with the director may have something to do with it."

739. Fargo is based in North Dakota.

740. No scene was shot in Fargo.

Fiddler on the Roof
(1971)

741.   Frank Sinatra turned down the role of Tevye.

742.   Norma Crane played Golde. She was dying of breast cancer throughout filming. Only three people on set knew about her illness.

743.   Topol was only in his thirties when he played the elderly character, Tevye.

744.   The film was surprisingly successful in Japan.

745.   The Sunrise, Sunset scene was created using hundreds of candles.

746.   The snow in the film is actually marble dust.

747.   Orson Welles was considered for Tevye.

748.   Topol played Tevye before in the London production of the stage musical.

749.   Katey Sagal auditioned for Golde.

750.   Norman Jewison was given the director' chair as the studio believed he was Jewish. When he met the executives, the first thing he said was, "You know I'm not Jewish... right?"

Fight Club
(1999)

751.   The director, David Fincher, says that there is a Starbucks coffee cup in every scene.

752.   It is ranked #10 on the top 250 best films on IMDB.

753.   When The Narrator punches Tyler Durden in the ear, Edward Norton actually punched Brad Pitt. You can see Norton laughing afterward.

754.   After Brad Pitt's parents saw the chemical burn scene, they stopped watching it. They have never seen the rest of the film.

755.   When a Fight Club member sprays the priest with a hose, the camera shakes because the cameraman couldn't stop laughing.

756.   Pitt and Norton were actually drunk during the golf ball scene.

757.   The film is based off the book by Chuck Palahniuk. He came up with the idea for the story when he got into a fight and went into work the next day looking battered and bruised. Nobody asked him about his injuries. He became obsessed with this "societal blocking" people have, which became the foundation of the novel.

758.   When Tyler Durden gives his speech, "We've all been raised on television to believe that one day, we'd all be millionaires and movie gods and rock stars," he looks at Jared Leto's character. Jared Leto created the band, 30 Seconds to Mars, in 1998.

759. Norton and Pitt took lessons in taekwondo, grappling and boxing to prepare for their roles.

760. Norton and Pitt studied UFC for hours.

761. Pitt had his front tooth chipped by a dentist for the role of Tyler Durden.

762. Helena Bonham Carter asked her makeup artist to apply makeup with her left hand so it would look sloppy.

763. Tyler Durden was supposed to have a scene where he explains how to build a home-made bomb but the director decided not to go along with it, worried that it would encourage people.

764. Brad Pitt was supposed to appear for a single frame during the 20th Century Fox logo, but the studio refused.

765. Meatloaf played Bob. His, fat suit weighed 100lbs.

766. Brad Pitt and Helena Bonham Carter's sex scene was done using the same Bullet-Time special effect used for The Matrix.

767. The studio had no idea how to market the film. Trailers emphasised the fighting segments (which are brief in the film.) Fincher was outraged when he saw the film being advertised during WWE and UFC.

768. Fincher felt like the penguin scene was necessary near the beginning to show the audience how weird the film was going to be.

769.   Brad Pitt and Edward Norton had to learn how to make soap to give their characters authenticity.

770.   Edward Norton lost 20lbs for the role.

The Fighter
(2010)

771.   Christian Bale lost 30lbs to play Dicky Eklund.

772.   Although Dicky is not portrayed in a good light, Dicky was well impressed with Bale's performance. However, he had an argument with Bale about the unflattering depiction of his family.

773.   Mark Wahlberg wasn't paid for the film.

774.   Martin Scorsese turned down the opportunity to direct.

775.   Brad Pitt was considered for the part of Dicky.

776.   The real boxers, Micky Ward and Dicky Eklund, were meant to have cameos but they declined.

777.   Michael Fassbender auditioned for a part.

778.   Emily Blunt turned down the lead.

779.   The interviews in the film were improvised by Christian Bale and Mark Wahlberg.

780.   There were 200 dummies in the audience of the climatic fight.

Finding Nemo
(2003)

781. Nemo first appeared in the film, Monster's Inc., in Boo's room.

782. Finding Nemo is the best selling DVD of all time with 40 million copies.

783. Crush says "dude" twenty-one times.

784. This was the first PIXAR film to win an Oscar for Best Animated Feature.

785. Marlin and Dory have opposite personalities. They also happened to be opposite colours.

786. William H. Macy was cast as Marlin and he recorded all of his lines. PIXAR believed that his voice wasn't right, so he was replaced with Albert Brooks.

787. Buzz Lightyear appears on the floor of the waiting room.

788. The mermaid in the aquarium tank was in Knick Knack, one of the first shorts PIXAR ever created in 1989.

789. PIXAR started working on the film in 1997. It wasn't released until 2003.

790. Mike from Monster's Inc. appears in the closing credits.

For a Few Dollars More
(1965)

791.   Although Clint Eastwood seems to be playing the same character as the one he portrayed in A Fistful of Dollars, he was not legally allowed to be called by the same name. In A Fistful of Dollars, his name is Joe. In this film, his name is Monco. In the sequel, The Good, the Bad and the Ugly, he is called Blondie.

792.   Clint's character's name, Monco, is derived from the Spanish word, Manco, which means "lame in one hand." This name suits Monco because he is always hiding one hand.

793.   This was the first Hollywood film to show a horse being shot down.

794.   This was one of the first Hollywood films to show a character using marijuana.

795.   Sergio Leone had no idea that he was breaking Hollywood's' rules when he showed a horse being shot or a character using drugs.

796.   This was the first Hollywood film to show the shooter and the victim in the same shot.

797.   Sergio Leone's films popularised characters tilting their guns to the side. Most films do this to "look cool." However, Leone said it was necessary so the audience could see the gun barrel and the face of the shooter simultaneously.

798.   Monco always has his right hand on his gun underneath his poncho.

799.   Leone didn't want to make this film. The studio forced him to or he wouldn't be paid for his previous film.

800.   The whistling heard in the opening credits was done by the director.

Forrest Gump
(1994)

801.   Tom Hanks ad-libbed the line, "My name is Forrest Gump. People call me Forrest Gump."

802.   This is the film debut of Haley Joel Osment. He play's Forrest's son.

803.   The film is based off the 1986 novel of the same name. It was written by Winston Groom.

804.   Winston Groom had a 3% share of the film's profits.

805.   Lieutenant Dan jokes about Forrest Gump becoming an astronaut. In the book's sequel, Gump and Co., Forrest becomes an astronaut.
Also, the following film Tom Hanks did was Apollo 13, where he played an astronaut.

806.   Tom Hanks wasn't paid for the film. He took a percentage of the profits and walked away with $40 million.

807.   In the book, Gump and Co., Forrest references how an inaccurate film was made about him but he got to meet Tom Hanks because of it.

808.   Tom Hanks was reluctant about playing Forrest Gump with a thick, Southern accent, believing that nobody really speaks like that. He changed his mind when he met Michael Humphreys, the actor who plays Forrest as a boy. The Southern accent Humphreys uses in the film is his actual accent.

809. All of the Ping-Pong balls that Gump hits were created with special effects. Tom Hanks was actually hitting nothing.

810. When Forrest Gump is told to "keep his eye on the ball" while he plays Ping-Pong, he never blinks in any scene where he plays Ping-Pong.

811. Bill Murray was considered for Forrest Gump.

812. Gary Sinise's lower legs were covered in bright blue fabric that allowed the special effects unit to remove them digitally.

813. In every still of Forrest Gump, he has his eyes closed.

814. The bench that Forrest sits on is now in the Savannah History Museum in Georgia.

815. Forrest's running scene was inspired by Louis Michael Figueroa who ran from New Jersey to San Francisco in 1982 when he was sixteen.

816. Demi Moore turned down the role of Jenny.

817. Kurt Russell does the voice of Elvis.

818. Although Sally Field plays Forrest Gump's mother, she is only ten years older than Tom Hanks.

819. The writer of Forrest Gump thought that John Goodman would've been the perfect actor to portray Forrest.

820. Terry Gilliam turned down the director's chair.

Frankenstein
(1931)

821.   Boris Karloff played The Monster. He was so unknown when he got cast that he wasn't invited to the film's premier.

822.   In the beginning of the film, the credits say that The Monster is played by ...?
He is credited at the end of the film.

823.   When The Monster is resurrected, a sound effect is used, which was known as Castle Thunder. This is the most famous Thunder sound effect in film history and has been used in thousands of films. This was the first film it was ever used for.

824.   Boris Karloff was considered a slow burner in Hollywood as he had starred in over seventy films before Frankenstein and was forty-four when he portrayed The Monster.

825.   In the novel, Frankenstein's first name is Victor. His name was changed to "Henry" for the film as "Victor" sounded too unfriendly.

826.   The shoes Boris Karloff wore as The Monster weighed 13lbs each.

827.   Although The Monster looks like he is over 7ft tall, Boris Karloff was only 5ft 11.

828.   Many people think that The Monster has bolts in his neck. They are actually electrodes.

829.   When The Monster is resurrected, Frankenstein says, "Now I know what it's like to be God!" When the

film was re-released, a thunder sound effect was played during this scene so it was inaudible. This was because the censor board thought this line was blasphemous.

830.   This film wasn't considered a horror film because the term "horror" as a film genre wasn't used until 1934.

Full Metal Jacket
(1987)

831.   At the time, Vincent D'Onofrio had the world record for putting on the most weight for a film when he piled on 65lbs to play Private Pile.

832.   It took Vincent D'Onofrio nine months to lose the weight he gained for this film.

833.   D'Onofrio tore ligaments in his knees due to his extra weight.

834.   Arnold Schwarzenegger was offered a role but he decided to do The Running Man.

835.   R. Lee Ermey plays Gunnery Sgt. Hartmann. However, he wasn't cast in the role originally. He was simply an advisor due to serving eleven years in the US Marine Corps and he eventually became a Gunnery Sergeant. He went up to Kubrick and insisted that only he could play the role. When Kubrick refused, Ermey barked for Kubrick to stand. The director obeyed immediately and gave Ermey the role.

836.   Kubrick rarely allows actors to improvise but he gave Ermey total freedom in his scenes since he was so creative with his obscenities.

837.   Ermey was not allowed to speak to anyone in-between takes.

838.   In some scenes, Ermey never moves his left arm. This is because he was involved in a jeep crash during filming and broke all of his ribs on the left side.

839.   One day, a herd of rabbits died near the set. Kubrick was so upset, that he cancelled the rest of the day's shoot.

840.   Gunnery Hartman almost never blinks throughout the film.

841.   Hartman is never seen without his hat.

842.   Despite Ermey's terrifying portrayal of Hartman, Ermey has stated that a drill instructor would never slap, punch or choke a recruit in front of other recruits under any circumstances. He never saw it happen in all of his years in the Marines.

843.   The actor, Matthew Modine, got married, had a child and celebrated his child's first birthday all during the film's shoot.

844.   Kubrick told Modine that he wasn't allowed to leave the set to see the birth of his child. After a heated argument, Kubrick allowed Modine to leave.

845.   Animal Mother's helmet says, "I Am Become Death." This is a quotation, famously said by J. Robert Oppenheimer after the first atomic bomb exploded.

846.   The second-half of the film was shot first.

847.   This was the first film Kubrick edited on a computer.

848.   The cast ate the same food and portions as the military did during the Vietnamese War.

849.   In the Vietnamese grave scene, there is a little girl with a camera. This girl is played by Stanley Kubrick's daughter, Vivian.

850.   A scene was cut where Hartman shows pride to the recruits for completing their training.

Gandhi
(1982)

851. Many Indians complained that Gandhi was portrayed by the English actor, Ben Kingsley. However, both of Kingsley's parents are Indian and are from the same state as Gandhi. Kingsley real name is Krishna Bhanji. He changed his name to "Kingsley" in honour of Gandhi, who stayed at Kingsley Hall when he travelled to London in 1931.

852. This is Daniel Day-Lewis' film debut.

853. Dustin Hoffman wanted to play the lead role.

854. 300,000 extras were used for the opening scene. This is the world record for the most extras in a single scene.

855. The director, Richard Attenborough, had to re-mortgage his house to fund the film.

856. Richard Attenborough's son, Michael, recommended Ben Kingsley for the title role.

857. Alec Guinness was strongly considered to play Gandhi.

858. Kingsley lived the same way as Gandhi throughout production. He would pray, fast and eat the same food and portions as Gandhi.

859. Martin Sheen donated his fee to charity.

860. The Indian government paid for 1/3rd of the budget.

The General
(1926)

861.   The scene where the train crashes through the bridge is the most expensive scene of the entire silent film era.

862.   When the train crashed into the river, it wasn't hauled out until World War II.

863.   The film cost $400,000.

864.   The film's look was inspired by Civil War photographs.

865.   Buster Keaton had to be extremely careful for the cannonball scene. To make sure the cannon blast would be exactly as powerful as he wanted it to be, he had to count how much gunpowder he put into the cannon with tweezers.

866.   This was the film Buster Keaton was proudest of.

867.   This is the shortest film to be ranked in the top 250 greatest films on IMDB. It is only sixty-seven minutes long.

868.   The film made very little money when it was released.

869.   The final battle scene caused a forest fire. The crew had to stop filming to put it out.

870.   During the train crash, a dummy was used for the engineer. It looked so realistic, that many people screamed in horror when the train crashed.

Gladiator
(2000)

871.   Joaquin Phoenix was only twenty-five when he played the villain, Commodus.

872.   Russell Crowe hated the film's dialogue. He despised the famous line, "I will have my vengeance, in this life or the next" and said to the writer, "Your lines are garbage but I'm the greatest actor in the world and I can make garbage sound good."

873.   Russell Crowe improvised a lot of his dialogue but none of it was used because he wasn't very good at it.

874.   Joaquin Phoenix improvised the famous line, "Am I not merciful?"

875.   Crowe's facial marks in the opening battle are real wounds he suffered when his horse backed him through tree branches.

876.   When a chariot collapses in one of the battle scenes, you can briefly see a gas canister spewing out smoke inside of it.

877.   Oliver Reed, who played Proximo in the film, died of a heart attack during the filming.

878.   When Maximus describes his home, it is the description of Russell Crowe's actual home in Australia.

879.   Oliver Reed hated Crowe upon meeting him. He even challenged Crowe to a fight while on set.

880.   Crowe said that Maximus is the best character he has ever played.

881.   Mel Gibson was offered the role of Maximus.

882.   In reality, Commodus ascended to the throne legally. He didn't live in the same time as Maximus.

883.   Oliver Reed took the part of Proximo because he wanted a "free trip to London to see a couple of shows."

884.   The masked gladiator, Tigris de Gaul, was supposed to be played by Lou Ferringo (who famously played the Incredible Hulk in the 1970s television show.)

885.   Despite what the gladiators look like in the film, most Roman gladiators were obese and they staged their fights. The masked gladiator, Tigris de Gaul, has the most accurate build of a gladiator.

886.   If you assumed the Coliseum was built to scale, you would be wrong. The director, Ridley Scott, visited the Coliseum and found it too small so he created a much larger version for the film.

887.   There was supposed to be a scene where Maximus fights a rhinoceros.

888.   400 cardboard cut-outs were used in the audience.

889.   Jude Law was nearly cast as Commodus.

890.   Jennifer Lopez auditioned for the part of Lucilla.

The Godfather
(1972)

891.   When Marlon Brando arrived on set in full makeup, a lot of the actors and crew didn't know who he was.

892.   The cat that Vito plays with at the start of the film was a stray that was found that morning.

893.   Robert De Niro auditioned for the part of Sonny. The director, Francis Ford Coppola, said it was the best audition he had ever seen. Nevertheless, Coppola believed that James Caan was more suited for the part and he got the role of Sonny.

894.   Jack Nicholson was the most the coveted actor to play Michael Corleone. The part went to Al Pacino, who was unknown at the time.

895.   It is currently #2 in the top 250 best films of all time on IMDB.

896.   Brando stuffed his face with cotton wool for the audition because he wanted Vito to look like a bulldog.

897.   Brando wore a mouthpiece for his character.

898.   When Michael pledges himself to Vito in the hospital, Brando started crying.

899.   The wrestler, Lenny Montana, was excited to do a scene with Marlon Brando. However, when he did the scene, he got so nervous, that he forgot his lines. The director kept this take in the film because it made Vito look powerful, watching a gigantic man shaking in his presence.

900. When Marlon Brando had to be carried from his bed down the stairs, he put weights under his body to make himself heavier. He didn't need to do this. He just wanted to annoy the cast. And he did.

901. Brando didn't learn most of his lines and read cue cards during his scenes.

902. Al Pacino refused to go to the Oscars after the release of this film because he was nominated for Best Supporting Actor even though he had more screen time than Marlon Brando (who had been nominated for Best Actor.)

903. Brando also boycotted the Oscars and allowed Sacheen Littlefeather (born as Maria Cruz) to represent him at the ceremony. When the presenter (Roger Moore) offered the Oscar to her, she snubbed him and read a speech talking about how the film industry is disrespectful to American Indians. She was booed off stage.

904. The studio hated Coppola and were desperately trying to have him fired.

905. Although Vito is often called "Don Corleone," this would never be said as an Italian term. He would be called by his first name so the term would be "Don Vito."

906. The film took sixty-two days to shoot.

907. Vito's distinct voice is based off mobster, Frank Costello. Frank Costello is also the name of Jack Nicholson's role in The Departed.

908. Sylvester Stallone auditioned for a role.

909.   Al Pacino was nominated for an Oscar for his performance in this film. It was the first of four consecutive Oscar nominations.

910.   Al Pacino got paid $35,000 for the part of Michael.

911.   Robert Duvall's wished the crew made a better wig for his character.

912.   The studio, Paramount, would have gone bankrupt if the film wasn't successful.

913.   Paramount asked Coppola to make the story as violent as possible, hoping this would encourage more people to see it.

914.   Brando was only forty-seven when he played Vito.

915.   There are sixty-one scenes of people eating.

916.   The studio wanted to have Coppola replaced with Elia Kazan.

917.   The colour orange foreshadows a tragedy in every scene.

918.   Coppola based many of the characters off his own family.

919.   Brando is in the film for less than an hour.

920.   Marlon Brando did a voiceover for The Godfather videogame. However, his voice was so unintelligible, that his dialogue couldn't be used and the game designers had to get a replacement.

The Godfather: Part II
(1974)

921.   Robert De Niro lived in Sicily for three months to prepare for his role.

922.   This is the first sequel to win an Oscar for Best Picture.

923.   The language that De Niro speaks isn't formal Italian. It's a combination of southern Italian dialects known as Sicilian.

924.   Nearly everything De Niro says is in Sicilian.

925.   It took De Niro four months to perfect the accent.

926.   The director, Francis Ford Coppola, started writing the script for this film the day The Godfather was released.

927.   Coppola was considering bringing Marlon Brando back to play Vito as a young man.

928.   The character, Merle Johnson, is played by Troy Donahue. By a complete coincidence, Troy's birth name was also Merle Johnson!

929.   The film claims to be based on the novel by Mario Puzo. However, the only parts of the film that are in the novel are the scenes with Vito.

930.   As of 2015, only five actors have won an Oscar for a role that was mainly in a foreign language – Mario Cotillard, Roberto Benigni, Benicio Del Toro, Sophia Loren and Robert De Niro for his role in this film.

931.   Although the word "mafia" isn't said once in The Godfather, it is said three times in this film.

932.   By the time this film came out, a lot of Italian mobsters started dressing, talking and acting like the characters from The Godfather (and still do.)

933.   Filming was delayed by a month when Al Pacino developed pneumonia.

934.   This film was green-lit before The Godfather was even released.

935.   Robert De Niro is the only actor to win an Oscar for taking over another actor's Oscar-winning performance.

936.   Al Pacino threatened to leave throughout the production due to impatience, bad dialogue and believing that he deserved more money.

937.   It was De Niro's idea for Vito to wrap his gun with a towel.

938.   Lee Strasberg came out of retirement to play Hyman Roth.

939.   Peter Sellers nearly got the part of Hyman Roth.

940.   Early reviews were negative as audiences found the flashbacks confusing.

Goldfinger
(1964)

941.   When Harold Sakata (who played Oddjob) chops James Bond, Sakata actually chopped him. You can see Sean Connery wincing in genuine pain.

942.   Harold Sakata was a Japanese-American weightlifter and professional wrestler.

943.   This was the first film to show a laser beam.

944.   In the original script, the laser was supposed to be a buzz saw.

945.   Orson Welles was considered to play Goldfinger.

946.   Goldfinger wears gold in every scene he is in except when he wears his military uniform.

947.   Sean Connery wears a toupee for this film… and every other Bond film he was in. He went bald when he was twenty-two.

948.   Sakata burned himself during his death scene. However, he didn't break the take until the director said "Cut!"

949.   Goldfinger was played by Gert Forbe. However, he was played by a different actor in the golf scenes as Forbe didn't know how to hold the club.

950.   All of Gert Forbe's lines are dubbed except, "No, Mr. Bond, I expect you to die" and "Except crime!"

The Gold Rush
(1925)

951.   This film is known as "the filmwhere Charlie Chaplin eats a boot." The boot was made of liquorice and Chaplin required sixty-three takes before he was satisfied. However, he was taken to hospital shortly after because he had consumed so much sugar that he was on the verge of developing lethal pancreatitis.

952.   The 2,500 prospectors were vagrants. They were hired for the day.

953.   This is the only film that Chaplin worked on where he had the entire story fully developed.

954.   This film was eventually released with narration. This was the first silent film that was changed into a sound film.

955.   The film was going to be called "Lucky Strike."

956.   This was Richard Attenborough's favourite film. He eventually directed the film, Chaplin.

957.   This was the first film that Chaplin starred in for United Artists.

958.   Most of the entire film was shot in a stage or a backlot.

959.   Chaplin's wife, Lita Grey, was intended for the lead but she couldn't be considered once she fell pregnant.

960.   During production, Chaplin's marriage with Lita Grey collapsed after he began an affair with leading lady, Georgie Hale.

Gone with the Wind
(1939)

961.   This was the first colour film to win an Oscar for Best Picture.

962.   Hattie McDaniel was the first African-American to be nominated and win an Oscar.

963.   Despite the fact Hattie made film history with her win for the film, she wasn't allowed to go to premier because she was black.

964.   This film is 238 minutes long, making it the longest film to ever win an Oscar for Best Picture.

965.   Vivien Leigh is in the film for 143 minutes. This means that she has the longest performance in a film to win an Oscar.

966.   The male lead, Clark Gable, hated the film and said it was "a woman's picture."

967.   This film is based off the 1936 book, Gone with the Wind. It won the Pulitzer Prize in 1937.

968.   The rights for the film were bought one month after the book was published.

969.   It received thirteen nominations.

970.   The studio wanted Katherine Hepburn to play Scarlett.

971.   During casting, the studio asked fans to vote for the actress they though should play the female lead, Scarlett. Vivien Leigh received a single vote.

972. The horse that Thomas Mitchell rides is the same horse that plays Silver in The Lone Ranger.

973. There was eighty-eight hours of footage after the film wrapped.

974. Judy Garland nearly played Scarlett's sister.

975. Michael Jackson bought the Best Picture Oscar this film received for $1.5 million.

976. The film was nearly called "Tomorrow is Another Day."

977. Clark Gable nearly quit when he learned that his character cries in one scene because he didn't want to come across as weak and effeminate.

978. George Cukor was supposed to be the director but he was fired.

979. Scarlett was originally going to be called Pansy.

980. The script changed every day. None of the cast received the final script until the film was finished.

981. Exactly half of the film takes place during the Civil War and the other half takes place afterward (during the Reconstruction.)

982. Vincent Price was considered for a role.

983. Errol Flynn nearly played the male lead.

984.   Gone with the Wind has more ticket sales than any film in American history. 200 million tickets were sold in America alone.

985.   The reason why the film did so well in the cinema is because it was very encouraging during World War II. It played in local cinemas for years worldwide throughout the war.

986.   F. Scott Fitzgerald was brought in to rewrite the script but he was fired.

987.   The line, "Frankly my dear, I don't give a damn" is often ranked at #1 in many polls for Greatest Movie Lines (including the poll done by the American Film Institute.)

988.   This is not the first film to say the word "damn." It was used in silent films and sound films such as Cavalcade in 1933.

989.   Some sources say that the producer was fined $5,000 for the film's usage of the word, "damn." This is not true.

990.   At first, the Hollywood Production Code (the company that dictates what is acceptable in a film) were uncertain whether the word "damn" would be deemed acceptable in the film. They considered the following alternatives –
"Frankly my dear, I don't give a hoot.
Frankly my dear, my indifference is boundless.
Frankly my dear, it makes my gorge rise."

The Good, the Bad and the Ugly
(1966)

991. It is ranked #8 in the top 250 greatest films ever on IMDB.

992. This is the highest rated film on IMDB that wasn't nominated for a single Oscar.

993. Blondie is "The Good," Angel Eyes is "The Bad" and Tuco is "The Ugly."

994. Ennio Morricone's iconic score was designed to sound like a crying hyena.

995. There is no dialogue for the first ten minutes and thirty seconds.

996. Eli Wallach has more screen time than Clint Eastwood.

997. The film was meant to be called "The Magnificent Rogues."

998. Orson Welles was adamant that this film would flop.

999. Charles Bronson was considered for the part of Tuco.

1000. When Tuco screams in Spanish, the literal translation is "Son of a bitch that gave birth to you!"

1001. Clint Eastwood was hesitant about doing the film, afraid that Tuco would upstage him.

1002.   Clint Eastwood only agreed to the film once he was paid $250,000 and given a Ferrari.

1003.   Clint Eastwood doesn't like this film.

1004.   Eli Wallach had to share a bed with Clint Eastwood during filming. He used to brag that he was the only man to sleep with Clint Eastwood.

1005.   In the train scene, you can see a step on one of the train carriages that passed by. The actor on set, Eli Wallach, had no idea that the train had an outward step. If he raised his head by a few inches in that scene, he would've been decapitated.

1006.   Mario Brega appears in all three of the Dollar films as the villain's henchman.

1007.   The skeleton that Tuco finds wasn't a prop. It was a real skeleton. It belonged to a Spanish actress that stipulated in her will that she wanted to act in death.

1008.   This film was the main inspiration for Stephen King's book series, The Dark Tower.

1009.   Eli Wallach barely spoke Italian and director, Sergio Leone, barely spoke English. They could only speak to each other in French.

1010.   A sequel for the film was considered.

Good Will Hunting
(1997)

1011.   Matt Damon and Robin Williams have a scene on the Boston Public Garden park bench. Since Robin Williams has died, the citizens of Boston leave flowers on the bench and write quotes from the film.

1012.   The painting that hangs in Sean Maguire's office was painted by the director, Gus Van Sant.

1013.   Mel Gibson was supposed to direct.

1014.   The studio was strongly considering removing Damon and Affleck and replacing them with Leonardo DiCaprio and Brad Pitt.

1015.   Matt Damon said that if Robin Williams didn't sign on for the film, it would've never been made.

1016.   Robin William's character is based off Matt Damon's mother and Ben Affleck's father.

1017.   Robin William's final line was ad-libbed.

1018.   This is the film that Matt Damon is proudest of.

1019.   Ben Affleck's brother, Casey, improvised nearly all of his lines.

1020.   Matt Damon and Ben Affleck wrote an extremely inappropriate scene in the original script. When the producer, Harvey Weinstein, mentioned it to Damon and Affleck, they said that the scene was only put in so they knew he actually read the script. Since he was the only person to ever mention it, it's a safe bet that no other studio actually read it.

Goodfellas
(1990)

1021.   The "Funny how?" scene actually happened to Joe Pesci when he tried to compliment a mobster

1022.   Al Pacino turned down the role of Jimmy Conway. The part went to Robert De Niro.

1023.   Joe Pesci played the terrifying Tommy DeSimone. Real friends of Tommy said that Pesci's portrayal is 99% accurate. The only difference was Tommy was tall and muscular, unlike Pesci who is 5ft 4.

1024.   Robert De Niro rang Henry Hill (who is played by Ray Liotta) seven or eight times a day to gain insight about his own character.

1025.   Ray Liotta's mother died during filming. He used the anger he had over her death in the famous pistol-whipping scene.

1026.   Some of the extras were played by real mobsters.

1027.   Ray Liotta turned down playing Harvey Dent in Batman for this film.

1028.   The previews for the film were the worst in the studio's history due to the violence.

1029.   The original title was "Wiseguy"

1030.   Marlon Brando encouraged Martin Scorsese not to make this film.

The Graduate
(1967)

1031.   Although Dustin Hoffman plays a college graduate, he was thirty at the time of shooting.

1032.   Robert Redford auditioned for the lead role.

1033.   The director, Mike Nichols, was paid a million dollars. This was the first time a director was paid this much.

1034.   Gene Hackman was cast as Mr. Robinson but was fired shortly after.

1035.   Judy Garland nearly played Mrs. Robinson.

1036.   Ronald Reagan was considered for Benjamin's father.

1037.   This was Christopher Reeve's favourite film.

1038.   Dustin Hoffman kept forgetting his lines during his audition. He was cast because his nervousness made him perfect for the role.

1039.   Dustin Hoffman was supposed to star in Mel Brooks', The Producers, before he was cast in this film.

1040.   Although Mrs. Robinson is supposed to be much older than Benjamin, there was only a six-year difference between the actors.

The Grapes of Wrath
(1940)

1041.   The director, John Ford, shot almost every scene in one take with no rehearsal.

1042.   This film is based off John Steinbeck's novel of the same name. He loved the film and said that Henry Fonda's portrayal as Tom Joad made him "believe my own words."

1043.   Steinbeck became such good friends with Fonda, that Fonda did a reading for Steinbeck's funeral.

1044.   The movie's fake title was "Highway 66."

1045.   Henry Fonda has the record for the longest gap between Oscar nominations. He was nominated for this film in 1940 and forty-one years later in On Golden Pond.

1046.   James Stewart was considered for a part.

1047.   The character of Noah disappears halfway through the movie. It is never explained what happened to him.

1048.   The producer, Darryl F. Zanuck, knew that Fonda was so desperate for the lead that he pretended he was going to give the part to another actor unless Fonda agreed to star in eight films with his studio.

1049.   The budget was $750,000.

1050.   This film was banned in the Soviet Union by Joseph Stalin because it showed that poor Americans' could still afford a car.

The Great Dictator
(1940)

1051. This was the first film with sound that Charlie Chaplin starred in.

1052. Hitler and a number of his associates watched the film twice in a private cinema. It is unknown what he thought of it. Chaplin said, "I'd give anything to know what he thought of it."

1053. Politician, Joseph McCarthy, said that this film undisputedly proved that Chaplin was a Communist.

1054. None of the German spoken in the film is real German.

1055. This film was banned in Germany until 1958.

1056. Chaplin said he would've never made this film if he knew of all of the atrocities that the Nazis committed.

1057. The film was financed entirely by Chaplin and it became his most successful film.

1058. Chaplin felt so uncomfortable every time he heard the Nazis committing evil acts in the news that he was compelled to shoot a happy ending that included the film's famous monologue.

1059. The film was shot over 539 days.

1060. The British government threatened to ban the film when Chaplin first announced it as they viewed the Nazi party as respected allies.

The Great Escape
(1963)

1061. Despite what many sources say, Steve McQueen did not perform the motorcycle jump in the film's climax. The stunt was performed by stuntman, Bud Ekins.

1062. Although the film is based off a true story, the motorcycle scenes are fictitious.

1063. McQueen only accepted the role if he was allowed to use his motorcycle.

1064. The story is based off the escape of Stalag Luft III on March 24th 1944. This date happened to be Steve McQueen's fourteenth birthday.

1065. Although the film is based off a historic event, all of the characters are fictional.

1066. None of the escapees from the actual Stalag Luft III were American like the film suggests.

1067. Charles Bronson played the chief tunneler. He got the part because he was a coal miner for years and he used his expertise for the role.

1068. Richard Harris was considered for a role.

1069. Donald Pleasance was an advisor due to his experience as a prisoner of war.

1070. The camp that the film is based in is in Sagan, Poland and can still be visited. The tunnel the prisoners used to escape is still there.

The Green Mile
(1999)

1071.   The film's writer, Stephen King, regularly visited the set. Tom Hanks stayed in character at all times in King's presence.

1072.   Tom Hanks plays Paul Edgecomb. He was supposed to play Edgecomb as an old man but the film crew couldn't make his makeup look right.

1073.   Doug Hutchison, who plays the villain, Percy, wore the squeakiest shoes he could possibly find for his character.

1074.   When Stephen King visited the set, he demanded to be strapped to the Old Spark (the electric chair.)

1075.   John Travolta was considered for the lead role.

1076.   Although all of the prison guards wear uniforms, death row guards didn't wear uniforms at the time the story is set.

1077.   Josh Brolin auditioned for the part of Wild Bill. The role went to Sam Rockwell.

1078.   The producers struggled to find an actor to portray John Coffey. It was Bruce Willis who suggested Michael Clarke Duncan after he had worked with him in the film, Armageddon.

1079.   Of the thirty films that were adapted from Stephen King's novels, this is the most successful.

1080.   Stephen King considers this film the most faithful adaption of all of his work.

Groundhog Day
(1993)

1081.   The concept of the story came from the writer, Danny Rubin, who was thinking how horrifying it would be to relive the same day over and over. He thought it would be even more frustrating if a person had to relive a holiday every day like Christmas or Halloween. He then tried to find the stupidest holiday possible for his main character to relive over and over. That is why he chose Groundhog's Day.

1082.   Harold Ramis was the director. He famously played Egon in Ghostbusters.

1083.   In one scene, Phil smashed the clock but it kept playing music. This wasn't a sound trick. The clock was genuinely still playing music even after it was bashed up.

1084.   All of the clocks in the diner are stopped.

1085.   Bill Murray was bitten repeatedly by the groundhog and had to have injections to avoid rabies.

1086.   The Groundhog announcer, Buster, is played by Bill Murray's brother, Brian.

1087.   Thirty-eight days are depicted in the film.

1088.   The film was originally going to conclude with Phil escaping the time loop but Rita becomes trapped in it.

1089.   Murray had a huge falling out with the director, Harold Ramis, and didn't speak to him for several years. After Ramis died, Murray said he was very immature during the film because he was going through a divorce and Ramis did nothing wrong.

1090.   Ramis cameos as the doctor that encourages Phil to see a psychiatrist.

1091.   The Swedish name for the film is "Monday All Week." The movie is set on a Tuesday.

1092.   Punxatawney became a massive tourist attraction after the film, which it still is to this day.

1093.   This was Michael Shannon's debut.

1094.   Bill Murray and Harold Ramis became grand marshals of the Groundhog day celebration in Punxsutawney.

1095.   The film was shot in Illnois, not Punxsutawney.

1096.   Phil's bedroom in the B & B was shot in a warehouse.

1097.   A group of groundhogs were raised during the production of the film.

1098.   Stephen Tobolowsky who plays Ned "Bing" Ryerson based his character off his own insurance agent.

1099.   In the original script, Phil is sentenced to relive the same day because of a curse placed upon him by a scorned lover.

1100.   In the original script, Phil is trapped in the time-loop for 10,000 days. That's over twenty-seven years.

Heat
(1995)

1101. Although this was the first time that De Niro and Pacino shared a scene, it wasn't the first film that they starred in together. They both starred in The Godfather: Part II but they were never in the same scene.

1102. Keanu Reeves was nearly cast as Chris. The role went to Val Kilmer.

1103. Pacino had a facelift just before filming.

1104. A video game was supposed to be made about the film but it was never completed.

1105. Nick Nolte nearly played the part that went to Pacino.

1106. Jeff Bridges nearly played the part that went to De Niro.

1107. This is Tom Hiddleston's favourite film.

1108. Jean Claude Van Damme was considered for a role.

1109. The film was shot in sixty-five locations. No soundstages were used.

1110. The famous diner scene with Pacino and De Niro was shot with no rehearsal.

High Noon
(1952)

1111.   This is Bill Clinton's favourite film.

1112.   The lead role was played by Gary Cooper. He suffered a bleeding ulcer throughout most of filming.

1113.   Gary Cooper wore no makeup to help show the character's age and fatigue.

1114.   Gregory Peck turned down the lead role of the film. He said it was the biggest regret of his career.

1115.   John Wayne hated this film.

1116.   High Noon is usually described as "a western for people who don't like westerns."

1117.   It took less than a month to shoot the film.

1118.   Henry Fonda was nearly cast as the lead.

1119.   The director, Fred Zimmerman, never took more than three takes of any scene.

1120.   Between takes, Gary Cooper would sleep under a tree.

The Hustler
(1961)

1121. Jake LaMotta plays a bartender in the film. LaMotta was a boxer who was famously portrayed by Robert De Niro in the biopic, Raging Bull. In this film, he says, "Check" three times.

1122. The director, Robert Rossen, was a pool hustler when he was younger.

1123. Pool became extremely popular nationwide after this film's release.

1124. Many of the film's extras are genuine street thugs.

1125. Tony Curtis turned down the lead role.

1126. Paul Newman had never played pool before being cast. He never even held a pool cue!

1127. This was one of the first Hollywood films to have a pre-credits scene.

1128. The film crew built a diner that looked so realistic, many people believed it was a real diner and would order food at the front desk.

1129. The film was nearly called "A Stroke of Luck."

1130. All of the pool shots are performed by the actors themselves.

The Imitation Game
(2014)

1131.   Winston Churchill said that the codebreakers depicted in this film made the biggest contribution to Britain's war effort.

1132.   Alan Turing was a world class distance runner. He ran a marathon in 2:46:03 in 1946.

1133.   Benedict Cumberbatch is related to his character, Alan Turing. They are seventeenth cousins!

1134.   Cumberbatch wore dentures that were modelled from Turing's teeth. No one told him to do this.

1135.   A New York Times reviews gave the film a PG-13 rating for its "violence and advanced mathematics."

1136.   Leonardo DiCaprio was considered for the lead.

1137.   One of Turing's relatives cameos as a dancer in the dance scene.

1138.   Mark Strong plays Stewart Menzies. Menzies inspired the character, M, for the James Bond series.

1139.   The double agent, Cairncross, never met Turing in real life.

1140.   In one of the final scenes, Turing learns that one of his workers, Cairncross, is a Soviet spy. Turing didn't turn him in because he knew that Cairncross would tell everyone that he is gay. This never happened and was only added in for dramatic effect.

However, if this did happen, Turing would've been sentenced to death for covering up for an enemy spy.

In the Heat of the Night
(1967)

1141.   Whoopi Goldberg said that when she saw the film in the cinema, the audience "lost their minds" when they saw a black man, Mr. Tibbs slap a white man.

1142.   Mr. Tibbs retaliation-slap to Endicott was improvised.

1143.   Rod Steiger had to chew gum in his scenes. Throughout production, he worked his way through 263 packs of gum.

1144.   George C. Scott was considered for a role.

1145.   The film had to be shot in the north because Sidney Poiter was nearly killed by the Ku Klux Klan when he visited Mississippi.

1146.   This is Danny Glover's favourite film.

1147.   This is the film that Sidney Poitier is proudest of.

1148.   The film was was shown in only a handful of cinemas in the South.

1149.   Rod Steiger maintained his Southern accent throughout the entire production.

1150.   Beah Richards stars in the film. She and Sidney Poiter also starred in Guess Who's Coming to Dinner?

In the Name of the Father
(1993)

1151.   Daniel Day-Lewis lost 30lbs for the role.

1152.   Day-Lewis spent many nights in jail to help get into the character.

1153.   Day-Lewis would encourage crew member to verbally abuse him and throw cold water at him.

1154.   Day-Lewis kept his Northern Irish accent for the entire shoot.

1155.   The story is based off the book, Proved Innocent, which is based off the true story of Gerry Conlon who was imprisoned for a crime he didn't commit.

1156.   In the credits, Giuseppe's name is misspelt as "Guiseppe."

1157.   Pete Postlethwaite and Daniel Day-Lewis were Oscar nominated but neither won.

1158.   Daniel Day-Lewis turned down the lead role in the film, Philadelphia, to star in this.

1159.   Although Pete Postlethwaite plays Daniel Day-Lewis' father, he was only eleven years older.

1160.   Bono was offered a role but he couldn't commit to the role due to touring.

Inception
(2010)

1161. When Christopher Nolan pitched the story to Warner Bros., they loved the idea and asked him to get back to them when he had a finished script. It took eight years for Nolan to write the script.

1162. The main character is called Dom. "Dom" is Slavic for "home." Dom obsesses about returning home for the entire film.

1163. The main characters require help from Yusuf in the film. "Yusuf" is the Arabic name for "Joseph." This is a reference to the Bible passage, Genesis 37-50, which details a man called Joseph who could interpret dreams.

1164. Dom's wife is called Mal. Her name is derived from the French word "malheur" which means "unhappy."

1165. Kate Winslet turned down the part of Dom's wife.

1166. Many complex scenes were created with absolutely no computer effects such as the Penrose stairs, the mountain avalanche, the zero gravity scene and the famous rotating hallway scene.

1167. When the film is shown on Japanese television, a reminder on the corner of the screen will say what dream level the characters are in.

1168. Michael Caine is only in the film for three minutes.

1169. The film's fake title was "Hour Glass."

1170.   This is the last film to be shot on film that won an Oscar for Best Cinematography. Every film since was shot digitally.

Indiana Jones and the Last Crusade
(1989)

1171.   George Lucas wanted the film to revolve around a haunted mansion.

1172.   It was Harrison Ford's idea for River Phoenix to play him as a teenager.

1173.   Gregory Peck was considered for the part of Indiana Jones' father.

1174.   2,000 rats were bred for the sewer scene.

1175.   When Indiana picks up the Holy Grail, he says, "That's the cup of a carpenter." Harrison Ford was a carpenter before he was an actor.

1176.   Spielberg considers this the best of the Indiana Jones films.

1177.   In the original script, Indiana Jones was going to journey to Africa and battle a Monkey prince.

1178.   Laurence Olivier was considered to play the Grail Knight.

1179.   Michael Sheard plays Hitler and Julian Glover plays the film's antagonist, Donovan. Both of these actors played villains in Star Wars: Episode V – The Empire Strikes Back.

1180.   The four horses at the end of the film were owned by King Hussein of Jordan.

Inglourious Basterds
(2009)

1181.   For years, Adam Sandler was strongly considered for the main part.

1182.   Only 30% of the film is in English.

1183.   The script took a decade to write.

1184.   Christoph Waltz speaks English, French, German and Italian in the film.

1185.   This was the first film directed by Tarantino to win an Oscar for acting. Christoph Waltz won an Oscar for Best Supporting Actor.

1186.   Anne Frank's name is carved into The Bear Jew's baseball bat.

1187.   Tarantino thought Diane Kruger was American when she came in to the audition for the German role, Bridget von Hammersmark. He had no idea she was German.

1188.   Jean Reno turned down a role.

1189.   Harvey Keitel is the voice of the American officer negotiating on the radio with Landa and Raine.

1190.   Tarantino has never explained why the title is misspelt.

Inside Out
(2015)

1191.   Each emotion is based off a shape – Joy is a star, Anger is a brick, Sadness is a tear, Fear is a nerve and Disgust is broccoli.

1192.   The writers were considering having up to twenty-seven emotions before they settled on five.

1193.   The original title was "State of Mind."

1194.   Disgust was originally envisioned as a male character.

1195.   Bing Bong's tail is based off the Cheshire Cat from Alice in Wonderland.

1196.   Four of the film's actors have played roles in the American version of The Office.

1197.   Joy is the only emotion that doesn't have a shadow.

1198.   Originally, Joy was supposed to enter the real world.

1199.   Originally, Riley was going to enter her own mind.

1200.   The film received an eight-minute standing ovation at its premier at the Cannes Film Festival.

Interstellar
(2014)

1201. Renounced astronomer, Kip Thorne, was brought in to ensure that everything in the script was possible or at the very least, theoretical. According to Thorpe, the ice clouds are the only things in the film that are scientifically impossible.

1202. The director, Christopher Nolan, grew 500 acres of corn for the film. When the corn scenes were finished, all of the corn was sold and Nolan made a profit.

1203. Anne Hathaway suffered hypothermia in the water scenes.

1204. Nolan cast Matthew McConnaughey as the lead after seeing his performance in the film, Mud.

1205. The dismantled robot on the ice planet is called KIPP. This is reference to Kip Thorne.

1206. Many of the shots of TARS are not computer-generated. In most shots, TARS is controlled by a puppeteer, who was digitally erased afterward.

1207. The film's fake title was "Flora's Letter."

1208. Matthew McConaughey's children, Levi and Vida, appear in the final scene.

1209. One of the astronaut's names is Hugh Mann (aka Human.)

1210. The word "interstellar" is only said once.

Into the Wild
(2007)

1211.   Emile Hirsch lost 40lbs for the role.

1212.   It took Sean Penn ten years to get approval to make this film.

1213.   Zach Galifianakis improvised all of his lines.

1214.   Originally, Sean Penn wanted Leonardo DiCaprio to play the lead.

1215.   Originally, Penn wanted Marlon Brando to play a part in the film.

1216.   The studio really wanted Shia LaBeouf for the lead.

1217.   Emile Hirsch did all of his own stunts.

1218.   The watch that Hirsch wear is the actual watch that his character, Christopher McCandless, wore.

1219.   When Hirsch did the scene where he was naked on the stream, the temperature was below freezing.

1220.   After the film's release, many people went out of their way to visit the area where Chris McCandless lived in the wild. Sadly, this resulted in several fatalities due to the area being near a violent river and a dangerous cliff.

It Happened One Night
(1934)

1221.   This was the first film to ever win an Oscar Grand Slam (Best Picture, Best Actor, Best Actress, Best Director and Best Screenplay.)

1222.   This was Joseph Stalin's favourite film.

1223.   The female lead was played by Claudette Colbert. She thought this would be the biggest flop of her career.

1224.   Colbert only accepted the role when the director doubled her salary.

1225.   It is often known as the first "screwball comedy."

1226.   This was the first film to win every major Oscar that it was nominated for.

1227.   The first thing Clark Gable said on his first day was, "Let's get this over with."

1228.   The was the first film to win both Best Actor and Best Actress.

1229.   Bette Davis was desperate to play the lead.

1230.   After Gable won the Oscar for this film, a child walked up to him and said he liked how shiny the award was. Gable gave it to the child and said that winning the award was more important than owning it. After Gable died, the child returned the Oscar to his family.

It's a Wonderful Life
(1946)

1231.   This film was a gigantic flop in its time.

1232.   The director, Frank Capra, said this was his best film.

1233.   Vincent Price was considered for a role.

1234.   The inspiration for the story came from a greeting card.

1235.   Howard Hughes nearly directed the film.

1236.   This film was forgotten until it started to be aired on Christmas Day. Soon after, it became known as a Christmas classic and one of the greatest films ever made.

1237.   James Stewart said this was his best film.

1238.   Although it's a Christmas film, it was shot in the summer.

1239.   Dalton Trumbo worked on the script. He was uncredited because he was publically declared as a member of the American Communist Party.

1240.   Forty-two rings are heard throughout the film. This means that forty-two angels have gotten their wings.

Jaws
(1975)

1241.   The shark is rarely seen because it kept malfunctioning.

1242.   Steven Spielberg called the shark, Bruce. Bruce was the name of Spielberg's lawyer.

1243.   This film is said to have been the first summer blockbuster.

1244.   The line, "You're gonna need a bigger boat" was unscripted.

1245.   Robert Shaw and Richard Dreyfuss hated each other throughout the shoot.

1246.   When Spielberg first heard John Williams' legendary score for the movie, he thought it was a joke.

1247.   The film is based off Peter Benchley's book of the same name. Benchley said that if he knew shark attacks were so rare, (about five a year worldwide,) he would've never written the story.

1248.   In the first public shark attack scene, you can see one extra laughing while everyone else is running around terrified.

1249.   There were three mechanical "Bruces" to play the shark. Each cost $250,000.

1250.   The film was supposed to be shot in fifty-two days. It took 150 days.

1251.   The author hated the ending.

1252.   Spielberg wanted Charlton Heston to play the lead.

1253.   Brody's dog was Spielberg's actual dog, Elmer.

1254.   A real shark was accidentally caught in a net while shooting the film. The footage of this shark was used for the film.

1255.   The producers said they would've never made the film if they knew how complicated the shoot was going to be.

1256.   Shark-fishing skyrocketed after the film's release.

1257.   Oliver Reed turned down the role of Quint.

1258.   Spielberg said the film wouldn't have been successful without the iconic music score.

1259.   Jon Voight was considered for the role of Hooper.

1260.   Jaw is directly responsible for a massive decline in package holiday trade.

Judgement at Nuremberg
(1961)

1261. This was Judy Garland's first film in seven years.

1262. Harrison Byers was played by William Shatner. He was unknown at the time, as the film was made five years before Shatner became famous for his role as Captain Kirk in the television show, Star Trek.

1263. William Shatner is the only cast member of this film that is still alive.

1264. Maximilian Schell won an Oscar for Best Actor. Since he was billed fifth, he is the lowest billed lead category winner in film history.

1265. Marlon Brando wanted to play Hans Rolfe.

1266. Montgomery Clift couldn't remember his lines so most of his dialogue was improvised.

1267. Laurence Olivier was supposed to play Ernst Janning.

1268. Marlene Dietrich had cosmetic surgery just before filming. Due to the surgery, her facial expressions were very limited and she grew to hate her performance in the film.

1269. Spencer Tracy was known for never working after 5pm. This is the only film where he didn't abide by this rule because he believed the subject matter was too important.

1270. Spencer Tracy's final monologue is eleven minutes long. It was done in one take.

Jurassic Park
(1993)

1271.   The writer, Michael Crichton, saw John Hammond as "a dark Walt Disney."

1272.   The T-Rex was not supposed to break the glass of the jeep. The screams of the children are genuine.

1273.   Shortly after the film's release, palaeontologists discovered that many dinosaurs had feathers, including the T-Rex and the Velociraptor.

1274.   The Velociraptors in the film bare little resemblance to real Velociraptors. Velociraptors were about ten-inches tall. The Velociraptors in the film closely resemble Utahraptors.

1275.   Crichton was paid $2 million for the rights to the novel before it was finished.

1276.   Harrison Ford was offered the lead part.

1277.   This was Richard Attenborough's first acting role in fourteen years.

1278.   It was common knowledge between palaeontologists before the film was released that the Brontosaurus and the Triceratops never actually existed. The "Brontosaurus" found a century ago was a fake and the "Triceratops" was a teenage Torosaurus.

1279.   When the Velociraptors enter the room that the children hide in, you can see a crew-member's hand push the dinosaur in.

1280. Jeff Goldblum's character, Ian, says, "Must go faster!" while the T-Rex chases him. He says the same line at the end of Independence Day.

1281. The sound of the T-Rex's footsteps are actually sequoia trees (the largest tree on Earth) crashing to the ground.

1282. The water ripple effect was caused by playing a guitar string directly below the plastic cup. Spielberg said this was the hardest effect to figure out, even more so than the dinosaur effects!

1283. The T-Rex was the largest robot ever constructed at the time of filming, measuring 20ft tall.

1284. Nearly everyone who died in the film, lives in the book and vice versa.

1285. The writer, Michael Crichton, said that 15% of the film was the same as his book.

1286. When the T-Rex grabs the Velociraptor during the climax, the Velociraptor disappears for a split-second. This was due to difficulties with the special effects.

1287. The sounds that the Brachiosaurus makes is a fusion of a whale and a donkey.

1288. Dinosaurs are only in the film for fifteen minutes.

1289. Jim Carrey was nearly cast as Ian.

1290. There is absolutely no explanation how the T-Rex entered the room at the end of the film (or how nobody noticed.)

Kill Bill: Vol. 1
(2003)

1291.   O-Ren taunts the Bride by saying, "You may not last five minutes." The fight is over in four minutes and fifty-nine seconds.

1292.   While Chiaki Kuriyama (Gogo) was shooting the scene where she hurls her ball-and-chain, she accidentally hit the director, Quentin Tarantino.

1293.   Uma Thurman said she was offered the part of The Bride from Tarantino as her 30th birthday present.

1294.   The man who plays the katana maker is Shin'ichi Chiba. He makes katanas in real life.

1295.   Jack Nicholson turned down the role of Bill.

1296.   Although The Bride's name is beeped out, her name can be seen on her plane ticket.

1297.   The Crazy 88 fight took two months to shoot.

1298.   The film starts with the proverb, "Revenge is a dish best served cold." This is a Klingon Proverb from the movie, Star Trek II: The Wrath of Khan.

1299.   Tarantino cameos as one of the Crazy 88 at the end of the fight when The Bride is admiring her handiwork.

1300.   Bill calls The Bride by her surname, Kiddo, in the beginning of the film. The audience doesn't realise that is her real name until the sequel.

Kill Bill Vol. 2
(2004)

1301. Quentin Tarantino was supposed to dub Pai Mei. He was going to do the dubbing intentionally bad, which was common in Asian films. This idea was eventually dropped.

1302. Tarantino nearly played Pai Mei. In the end, he was played by Gordon Liu (who also played Johnny Mo in Kill Bill Vol. 1.)

1303. Robert Rodriguez scored the film for $1.

1304. Pai Mei's three-inch punch is a reference to Bruce Lee's three-inch punch.

1305. The fight choreographer, Woo-Ping Yuen, was nearly cast as Pai Mei.

1306. Three out of the six members of the Deadly Viper Assassination Squad aren't named after vipers.

1307. The final fight was supposed to be on the beach under the moonlight but the production ran too long and the scene was cut.

1308. Daryl Hannah improvised the scene when she loses her eyes to make Tarantino laugh. She didn't realise he would put it in the final film.

1309. Darly Hannah sustained many injuries after she freaks out in Budd's caravan.

1310. The Bride never speaks to Budd.

The Killing
(1956)

1311. The film was hated upon its original release.

1312. This was Kubrick's third film and is considered to be his first masterpiece.

1313. This film heavily inspired non-linear stories like Pulp Fiction and Reservoir Dogs.

1314. Kubrick wasn't paid for this film.

1315. Frank Sinatra wanted to play a role in the film.

1316. This was the film debut of Rodney Dangerfield.

1317. The art director was Ruth Sobotka, Kubrick's wife.

1318. The film was shot in twenty-four days.

1319. The film was made for $320,000.

1320. Kirk Douglas loved the film so much that he pursued Kubrick to be a part of his next film. Kubrick's follow up was Paths of Glory, with Douglas as the lead.

King Kong
(1933)

1321.   Kong's roar was created by combining the roar of a tiger and a lion and then rewinding it slowly.

1322.   The T-Rex's hiss was from a puma.

1323.   The original title was "The Beast."

1324.   This film's sequel, Son of Kong, came out the same year.

1325.   12,000 people had to be turned away when the film premiered.

1326.   Kong doesn't appear for forty-seven minutes.

1327.   A scene involving a Spider Pit was cut from the film. However, Peter Jackson recreated it as a DVD extra for his 2005 film, King Kong.

1328.   The film begins with an "Old Arabian Proverb." This "proverb" was made up by the director.

1329.   Merian C. Cooper was the director. The first image he had of the story was a gigantic ape on top of a skyscraper fighting airplanes. He worked backwards from that.

1330.   This was Adolf Hitler's favourite film.

The King's Speech
(2010)

1331.   This film's screenplay was in the Blacklist; a list of excellent scripts that have yet to be made. It had existed for years Tom Hooper decided to direct it.

1332.   Paul Bettany was offered the part but he turned it down.

1333.   In the film, Lionel Logue is an actor who turns into a speech therapist. King George is played by Colin Firth, whose sister, Katie, is an actor who turned into a speech therapist.

1334.   This was an Australian co-production. It is the first Australian film to ever win an Oscar for Best Picture.

1335.   David Seidler was seventy-three when he won the Best Original Screenplay Oscar. He is the oldest person in history to win this Oscar.

1336.   Geoffrey Rush's and Colin Firth's characters discuss Shakespeare in the film. Both of them starred in Shakespeare in Love. In that film, Mark Williams played an actor with a terrible stutter.

1337.   The King's speech is not exactly the same as King George's speech in real life. The film's version is shorted by a third.

1338.   Guy Pearce is Australian but he plays a Brit. Evan Best is a Brit but she plays an American. Jennifer Ehle is American but she plays an Australian.

1339.   Although Guy Peace plays the older brother of Colin Firth's character, he is seven years younger than Firth.

1340.   The movie was written by David Seidler. He stammered as a child but was inspired when he heard King George VI's war speech. When he was an adult, he wrote to George's wife and asked her if he had permission to write a film about his story. She said he could after he passed away. He agreed.

Lawrence of Arabia
(1962)

1341.   Even though the movie is 227 minutes long, there is no dialogue from a female character. This is the longest film ever to have no dialogue spoken by a woman.

1342.   The director, David Lean, didn't get his money for the film for sixteen years.

1343.   Peter O' Toole had a scene where he walks down a staircase with Allenby. However, some of this scene had to be reshot a year later. Peter O' Toole has said on The Tonight Show that he is one year older at the bottom of the stairs than he is at the top.

1344.   Marlon Brando nearly played the lead character.

1345.   Peter O' Toole was considered too pretty to play Lawrence. Writer, Noel Coward said, "If he'd been any prettier, they'd have had to call it Florence of Arabia."

1346.   It took fourteen months to shoot the film. It then spent another two years in pre-production.

1347.   Almost every movement in the film is from left to right. The director did this to make the film feel like a journey.

1348.   Alec Guinness plays Faisal in the film. He has played T.E. Lawrence in Terence Rattigan play, Ross.

1349.   The Aqaba scene required 450 horses and 150 camels.

1350.   Peter O' Toole didn't see the film for twenty years.

L.A. Confidential
(1997)

1351.   This film is based off the neo-noir novel by James Ellroy. Ellroy is so good at writing crime novels because he used to be a criminal himself and spent many years in jail.

1352.   Guy Pearce had to spend time with a real cop to understand how L.A. police officers act. Pearce said that he couldn't stand the cop because he was so racist.

1353.   Michael Madsen was supposed to play Bud White. The part went to Russell Crowe.

1354.   At the time this story takes place, no building was allowed to be taller than city hall. The film crew had to be very specific where they placed their cameras to give the illusion that city hall was taller than any other structure.

1355.   Guy Pearce was in the audience when the writer, James Ellroy, announced that the film had gone into pre-production with two Australian actors playing the leads. The audience burst out laughing, believing that Ellroy was joking. Pearce felt humiliated.

1356.   James Ellroy thought Kevin Spacey was the best actor in the film.

1357.   Russell Crowe's character, Bud, was described as being "the biggest cop in the force." To make himself feel bigger, Crowe moved into a tiny apartment. He spent so much time ducking under doorways, that he felt 7ft tall.

1358.   Crowe got cast as Bud after the director saw him play the Neo-Nazi, Hando, in Romper Stomper.

1359.   Kim Basinger was the only actress considered for the part of Lynn.

1360.   Many of the scenes are based off real events including the beginning scene where the drunk police officers beat up the Hispanic prisoners.

La Dolce Vita
(1960)

1361.   This film coined the term "paparazzi."

1362.   According to the director, Federico Fellini, "paparazzi" means "sparrows" in Italian. This was the name he gave to photographers because they kept hopping and scurrying around celebrities like little birds.

1363.   This was film critic, Roger Ebert's, favourite film.

1364.   Paul Newman was considered for the lead role.

1365.   Henry Fonda was considered for Steiner.

1366.   The producer quit when Fellini said he wouldn't cast Paul Newman as the lead.

1367.   The Vatican voiced how much they despised this film due to its portrayal of Rome.

1368.   La Dolce Vita was banned in Spain until 1981.

1369.   Marcello Mastroianni had to stand in a freezing fountain for hours. He was so cold, he had to wear a wetsuit underneath his costume and drink an entire bottle of vodka.

1370.   Green dye had to be put in the fountain as the water looked too dirty.

Leon
(1994)

1371.   Natalie Portman was only eleven when she auditioned for the part of Mathilda. Mathilda was supposed to be fourteen so Portman was told she was too young. Although she was the youngest person to audition, she got the part.

1372.   Jean Reno played Leon as if he was mentally challenged. Since the little girl, Mathilda, loves him, he thought the audience would only believe he was not taking advantage of her if he wasn't mentally capable of doing so.

1373.   This was Natalie Portman's debut.

1374.   Gary Oldman famously overacts the line, "Bring me everyone. EVERYONE!" He did this as a joke to make the director laugh. This was the take that made it into the film.

1375.   Jean Reno played a similar character in the film, Nikita. Reno played a hitman called Victor the Cleaner. The director, Luc Besson, realised that the character was underused and wanted to develop him in another story. That idea turned into this film.

1376.   Gary Oldman's character, Stansfield, listens to Beethoven. Gary Oldman played Beethoven in the film, Immortal Beloved. It was released two months after Leon.

1377.   Liv Tyler was strongly considered for the part of Mathilda.

1378.   In the original script, Leon's surname is Montana.

1379.   Keith A. Glascoe played Stansfield's large henchman, Benny. He was one of the fireman who died during the collapse of the World Trade Centre on 9/11.

1380.   While the final scene was being filmed, a robbery occurred near the set. The thief ran onto the set and saw all of the extras wearing police uniforms. He assumed he was caught stealing and gave himself up.

Life is Beautiful
(1997)

1381.   When the actor and director, Roberto Benigni won the Oscar for Best Foreign Film, he was so happy, he jumped from chair to chair to get to the stage.

1382.   Benigni's character is Guido. Guido's wife is played by Benigni's wife, Nicoletta Braschi.

1383.   This is the second film in Oscar history to be nominated for Best Film and Best Foreign Film. The other was the 1969 film, Z.

1384.   This is the second Italian film to win a Best Actor Oscar. The other was Sophia Loren for the 1960 film, Two Women.

1385.   Life is Beautiful was nominated for seven Oscars.

1386.   Life is Beautiful was inspired by Benigni's father, Luigi, who was a concentration camp prisoner.

1387.   Benigni is the sixth actor ever to win a Best Actor Oscar for a comedy.

1388.   After this film received its nominations, he met the Italian President, Oscar Luigi Scalfaro. While he shook Oscar's hand, "Now I have the Oscar in my hand."

1389.   The title comes from Leon Trotsky. Before he was to be killed by Stalin's assassins, he saw his wife in the garden and wrote down, "In spite of everything, life is beautiful."

1390.   He and Laurence Olivier are the only actors to have directed themselves in Oscar winning performances.

Life of Brian
(1979)

1391.   The film was almost entirely funded by the Beatles singer, George Harrison.

1392.   George Harrison cameos as Mr. Papadopolous, owner of The Mount.

1393.   George Harrison's accent was so indecipherable that he was dubbed by Michael Palin.

1394.   Originally, Brian was supposed to be the thirteenth Apostle who kept missing the vital moments of Christ e.g. Lazarus/ The Last Supper, etc.

1395.   John Cleese was wearing clothes in the final Cross scene because he was so cold.

1396.   John Cleese desperately wanted to play Brian.

1397.   The tagline for the film was, "The film that is so funny that it was banned in Norway!"

1398.   John Cleese wanted former James Bond actor, George Lazenby, to play Christ.

1399.   The only character to appear in all four Python film is God.

1400.   Six actors played forty characters in this film.

Life of Pi
(2012)

1401.   M. Night Shyamalan nearly directed this film.

1402.   Pi was played by Suraj Sharma. This is his film debut. He beat 3,000 other actors for the part. He only went to the audition to support his brother.

1403.   The tiger is called Richard Parker. This is the name of Peter Parker's father in the film, The Amazing Spider-Man. This film stars Irrfan Khan... who also happens to star in THIS film as Pi when he is an adult!

1404.   Tobey MacGuire originally played the Writer. However, the part was recast because the director thought MacGuire would be too distracting because he is such a big star.

1405.   The studio that created the special effects for the film went bankrupt immediately after the film was released.

1406.   Pi reads The Mysterious Island by Jules Verne. He visits a mysterious island later in the film.

1407.   Ang Lee hired Steven Callahan as a consultant. He was trapped on a lifeboat for seventy-six days in 1982.

1408.   Ang Lee cameos in the queue behind Pi's mother receiving food from the cook.

1409.   The island is shaped like the Hindu God, Vishnu.

1410.   Pi is stuck on the lifeboat for 227 days. As a fraction, pi is 22/7.

The Lion King
(1994)

1411.   This film has the highest rating on IMDB of any Disney film.

1412.   Matthew Broderick played Simba as an adult. Nathan Lane played Timon. They only met once during the film's entire production.

1413.   Nathan Lane was supposed to play a hyena.

1414.   Liam Neeson was considered for Mufasa.

1415.   This was Gregory Peck's favourite animated film and one of his favourite films ever.

1416.   Originally, Rafiki was meant to be a cheetah.

1417.   At one point, Scar was going to be an evil baboon.

1418.   Disney animators ventured to Africa to study how the animals interacted with each other.

1419.   An adult lion and cub were brought into the studio so the animators could study their muscle structure and anatomy.

1420.   This is the most successful VHS film of all time.

1421.   Simba's parents are played by James Earl Jones and Madge Sinclair. They played a married couple in the film, Coming to America.

1422.   Although Nala's mother's name is never mentioned, it is Sarafina.

1423. Only three Disney films have ever won a Golden Globe for Best Picture – this, Toy Story 2 and Beauty and the Beast.

1424. Joe Pesci was offered the part of Timon.

1425. Tim Curry and Malcolm McDowell were considered for Scar.

1426. The film's original title was "King of the Jungle."

1427. Patrick Stewart was considered for Zazu.

1428. Many characters were cut from the original script including a rhino with a bird that lived on its back, a bat-eared fox called Bhati, Nala's father and her brother, Mheetu, a meerkat besides Timon and a rock python called Joka.

1429. The hyenas are the animals that resemble the creatures they are based on the most.

1430. 600 artists worked on the film.

Lock, Stock and Two Smoking Barrels
(1998)

1431.   This was Jason Statham and Vinnie Jones' film debut.

1432.   The director chose Jason Statham for the role of Bacon because he knew Statham used to be a street vendor and would be more believable than an actor.

1433.   Lenny McLean played Barry the Baptist. The film is dedicated to him as he died of lung cancer a month before the film was released.

1434.   Lenny Lean used to be a bare knuckle boxer.

1435.   Ray Winstone was offered the part of Hatchet Harry.

1436.   The director of Kick-Ass and Kingsman, Matthew Vaughn, cameos as a guy dragged out of the car by Dog.

1437.   Supermodel, Claudia Schiffer, was cast in the film but she was eventually edited out.

1438.   Nick the Greek is sometimes called Nick the Bubble. This is cockney slang for the meal, bubble and squeak, which means Greek.

1439.   When Nick is arguing to Tom, Nick says, "All right, keep your Alans on!"
This is a reference to the British journalist, Alan Whicker. It was cockney slang for "knickers."

1440.   Vinnie Jones was released from police custody for beating up his neighbour on his first day of filming.

The Lord of the Rings: The Fellowship of the Ring
(2001)

1441.   Sean Connery was offered the part of Gandalf the Grey. He turned it down because he didn't understand the script. The studio was so sure the film would fail without him, they offered him a huge percentage of the movie's profit. However, Connery didn't want to spend years in New Zealand so he rejected the role to work on the film, The League of Extraordinary Gentlemen. The film turned out so badly, that it encouraged Connery to quit acting forever. If he accepted the role of Gandalf, he would've been paid $560 million. That would've been, by far, the most any actor has ever been paid for a film.

1442.   Christopher Lee was desperate to play Gandalf the Grey. However, the studio found him to be too old for the part. He was cast as the villain, Saruman.

1443.   Christopher Lee was the only person who worked on The Lord of the Rings films to have met the writer, J.R.R. Tolkien.

1444.   Lee has read The Lord of the Rings every year from the day it was published until the year of his death.

1445.   Lee is fluent in Elvish and several fictitious languages from the stories. When Saruman casts a dark spell on the Fellowship, none of the film crew told Christopher Lee what to say in that scene. He knew the exact enchantment he needed to say.

1446.   At the end of the film, Aragorn deflects a dagger that is thrown at him by the Uruk-Hai, Lurtz. This was an accident. The actor who portrays Lurtz, Lawrence Makoare, was suppose to throw the dagger at a tree but he accidentally hurled it at Viggo Mortensen. Also, this was a real dagger. Luckily, Viggo deflected it in time.

1447. When Gandalf challenges the Balrog, Ian McKellen was actually acting to a Ping-Pong ball.

1448. Ironically, the actor who plays Gimli the dwarf, John Rhys-Davies, was the tallest of the Fellowship. He is 6ft 1.

1449. When Bilbo drops the One Ring on the floor at the beginning of the film, the Ring doesn't bounce. This was done by making the surface magnetic.

1450. Orlando Bloom was cast as Legolas two days before he finished drama school.

1451. Sean Astin, who plays Samwise, severely cut his foot for his final scene when he runs into the water towards Frodo. He stepped on a shard of broken glass and needed immediate medical attention.

1452. Viggo Mortensen joined the film while they were already shooting. He hadn't read the books nor did he meet the director, Peter Jackson. He replaced Stuart Townsend who was considered too young for the part.

1453. The swordsman who played Darth Vader in Return of the Jedi, trained Viggo Mortensen for his role as Aragorn. He said that Viggo was "the best swordsman I've ever trained."

1454. If this film didn't succeed, it would've bankrupted the studio.

1455. Ian McKellen's voice as Gandalf is based off J.R.R. Tolkien.

1456.   Peter Jackson cameos as a man eating a carrot outside the Prancing Pony.

1457.   John Rhys-Davies was allergic to his make-up and would suffered inflammation around his eyes upon wearing it. It was so painful, he couldn't work two days in a row. When all of the films wrapped, each principal actor gave a speech except Davies. Instead of giving a speech, he just ran into the room, grabbed his character's mask and threw it in the fire.

1458.   In the Prancing Pony, some of the actors are on stilts to make the Hobbits look smaller.

1459.   Christopher Lee was the first to be cast because of his gargantuan knowledge of the series.

1460.   Sean Astin gained 30lbs for the part of Samwise.

1461.   Viggo Mortensen always kept his sword with him. He was nearly arrested several times.

1462.   It took two months for Orlando Bloom to learn how to use a bow and arrow.

1463.   The Orc blacksmiths were played by the staff who created the Orc weapons.

1464.   Ian McKellen genuinely whacked his head off the ceiling of Bilbo's house. His reaction was real.

1465.   19,000 costumes were made for the film.

1466.   The moth that Gandalf speaks to was born that day and died hours later.

1467.   When Gandalf leaves The Shire to research The Ring, it seems like he leaves for a few weeks or months. In the book, he researches The Ring for seventeen years.

1468.   The Orcs cries are the nocturnal screams from possums.

1469.   J.R.R. Tolkien's son, Christopher, detests all of The Lord of the Rings films.

1470.   So much chainmail had to be made for this film and the sequels, that the crew members who created them wore their fingerprints off their fingers.

The Lord of the Rings: The Two Towers
(2002)

1471.   John Rhys-Davies, who plays the dwarf, Gimli, is missing the tip of his finger and required a prosthetic fingertip for the film. One day, he put fake blood on the prosthetic and showed it to Peter Jackson and pretended his finger was holding on by a thread. Jackson freaked out and demanded that Davies be taken to a hospital. For someone who created gory films like Bad Taste and Braindead, he's surprisingly squeamish.

1472.   When Gandalf calls his horse, Shadowfax, the horse galloped to him on the first take.

1473.   When Gollum is eating a fish, the actor, Andy Serkis, is actually eating a fish-shaped lollipop.

1474.   Andy Serkis was only supposed to do three-weeks voiceover work for this film. However, Jackson loved how Serkis distorted his whole body in the audition and said he had to play the physical Gollum as well.

1475.   Although the Uruk-Hai are supposed to be tall, Jackson had such difficulty finding tall actors that some of them are only five foot. They were known as Uruk-Lows.

1476.   Almost none of the actors who played the Uruk-Hai are big or muscular. They were just normal people wearing muscular costumes. The costumes were destroyed every day and new ones had to be built the day after.

1477.   Animators created many computer-generated soldiers for the Helm's Deep battle. Each of the soldiers were given a set list of things to do (some threw spears, some would focus on the defensive, some would protect others, etc.) The first time they ran the program, half of the Helm's Deep soldiers ran away from the Uruk-Hai.

1478.   Andy Serkis based Gollum's desperation on a heroin addict suffering withdrawal.

1479.   Andy Serkis drank a concoction of honey, lemon and ginger so he wouldn't lose his voice as Gollum. The concoction was called Gollum Juice.

1480.   Gollum's real name is Smeagol. When he reverts to Smeagol, he has wide pupils. When he is Gollum, he has narrow pupils like a predatory animal.

1481.   Andy Serkis did the voice of the three Orcs arguing over whether or not they should eat the Hobbits.

1482.   It took eight minutes to render one frame of Gollum. It took two days to render one frame of Treebeard.

1483.   Treebeard's voice and manner of talking is based of C.S. Lewis, the writer of The Lion, the Witch and the Wardrobe. He was good friends with J.R.R. Tolkien, the writer of The Lord of the Rings.

1484.   Orlando Bloom auditioned for Faramir.

1485.   In the extended version, Aragorn reveals that he is eighty-seven years old. This is because he is a descendent of the Dunedain, who are gifted with long life.

1486.   The book concludes with Frodo confronting the giant spider, Shelob. However, Jackson wasn't sure at first whether he should include her in this film or the next one. He built the set for Shelob's Lair just in case. When he realised that Shelob would have to wait until the next film, he had to leave her Lair in a warehouse for a year.

1487.   None of the Uruk-Hai have armour on their back because Saruman believed they would never run away from battle.

1488.   The Orcs have black blood. When blood seeps out of their mouths, the Orc actors would spew out liquid-liquorice.

1489.   Peter Jackson cameos as a Helm's Deep fighter hurling a spear.

1490.   When Viggo Mortensen kicks the helmet near the Orc pyre, he screamed because he broke two of his toes.

1491.   The Helm's Deep scene took four months to shoot, every single night.

1492.   Jackson needed so many Rohirrim riders, that many of them are women with glued-on beards. Jackson said the women were better horse-riders than men.

1493.   The staff-stomping the Uruk-Hai do before battle was unscripted. One of the actors started doing it out of boredom, in between shots and the rest of the actors joined in.

1494.   Andy Serkis said that his favourite scene from the entire Lord of the Rings trilogy is when Samwise cooks the rabbits that Gollum finds.

1495.   Andy Serkis found the rock-climbing scene quite easy as he had done rock-climbing for years.

1496.   Brad Dourif played Grima Wormtongue. His daughter is called Arwen. Arwen is the name of Liv Tyler's character in the film.

1497.   When Gandalf first appears as Gandalf the White, his voice is a combination of Ian McKellen and Christopher Lee.

1498.   There were never more than 100 Uruk-Hai in any scene.

1499.   Andy Serkis based the sound, "Gollum! Gollum!" off a cat coughing up a hairball.

1500.   When Frodo, Samwise and Gollum see the Gates of Mordor, it is shot exactly the same as the scene in The Wizard of Oz, when the group arrive at the Witch's Lair.

The Lord of the Rings: The Return of the King
(2003)

1501.   Many people complain that the Eagles should've just flown the One Ring straight to Mount Doom in the first place. According to the book, this wasn't possible because they would've been corrupted by the Eye of Sauron, which is near the mountain. The Eagles would've been compelled to fly straight to Sauron's castle and he would've reclaimed his power.

1502.   This film is ranked the highest on IMDB of the LOTR trilogy. It is #9 on IMDB's top 250 greatest films ever made.

1503.   Viggo Mortensen finds this film overrated due to the excessive special effects.

1504.   Although the Hobbits call the tusked creatures Oliphaunts, they're called Muma-Kils.

1505.   Aragorn was supposed to fight Sauron in the final battle. Although this scene was shot, Sauron was replaced by an armour-clad troll. You can still watch the Sauron fight on the extras on the DVD.

1506.   In the extended version, the Fellowship is confronted by the Mouth of Sauron. In this scene, the Mouth taunts the heroes by telling them that Frodo has died. This scene was cut because the audience knew that Frodo was still alive so it wouldn't be a dramatic scene. At this point in the book, the reader believed that Frodo was dead.

1507.   J.R.R. Tolkien hated the title for this story because he believed it spoiled the ending. He wanted to call it "The War of the Ring."

1508.   Viggo Mortensen said that during the course of filming the trilogy, he had killed every stuntman fifty times.

1509.   Jackson personally hates the Army of the Dead in the story but he had to include it for the diehard fans.

1510.   Jackson's cameo can only be seen in the extended version. He appears as a pirate.

1511.   The very last shot that the filmmakers did was the destruction of the One Ring.

1512.   The trilogy is the most nominated film series in Oscar history.

1513.   This is the first film in history to be the third film in a series to win an Oscar for Best Picture.

1514.   This is the first sequel to win an Oscar for Best Picture since The Godfather: Part II.

1515.   Bernard Hill plays Theoden. He also played the captain in Titanic. This means that he has starred in two films that won eleven Oscars.

1516.   Bernard Hill has appeared in three films that won Best Picture and Best Director – Gandhi, Titanic and this.

1517.   This is the first fantasy film to ever win the Oscar for Best Picture.

1518.   It has the highest perfect score in Oscar history because it had eleven nominations and won every one of them.

1519.   The entire franchise won every Oscar it was nominated for (thirty) apart from one.

1520.   The film was finished five days before its premiere. Many crewmembers were certain the film would be delayed.

1521.   Shelob the spider's cries are from a steam train hissing combined with the shriek of a Tasmanian Devil.

1522.   Christopher Lee was so angry that his scene was cut, that he refused to go to the premier. Many fans thought his reaction was justified.

1523.   Shelob is based off the New Zealand funnel web spider.

1524.   Jackson wanted Daniel-Day Lewis to play Aragorn.

1525.   Andy Serkis does the voice of the Witch-King. He is played by Lawrence Makoare, the same actor who played Lurtz the Uruk-Hai in the first film.

1526.   Lawrence Makoare also played Gothmog, the Orc leader. Actors kept forgetting the character's name so they called him Pimplehead.

1527.   John Rhys-Davies auditioned for the part of Denethor.

1528.   When Jackson asked Christopher Lee to imagine what it would be like to be stabbed in the back, Lee said, "I don't have to imagine. I know." Lee was a Nazi spy and solider during World War II.

1529.   To make computer-generated horses look realistic, horses had to wear motion-capture suits.

1530.   Peter Jackson jokes that The Return of the King is the first movie to win an Oscar for Best Picture before it was finished. The day after he won the Oscar, he had to finished the extended cut for the DVD.

M
(1931)

1531.   The director, Frtiz Lang cast real criminals for the court scene. Twenty-four of them were arrested during filming.

1532.   The original title was "The Murderers Are Among Us."

1533.   There is a misconception that the title was changed because Lang wasn't allowed to use the word "Murder" in the title.

However, Lang changed the title to "M" because he found it more powerful when the criminal writers the letter, M, on his hand.

1534.   Nazis banned the film in Germany in 1934. Germans couldn't see the film until 1966.

1535.   The whole film was shot in six weeks.

1536.   Lang said this was his best film.

1537.   The use of voiceover narration in the film was a new film technique at the time.

1538.   Nazi propagandist, Joseph Goebbels, loved the film as it was "free of phony humanitarian sentiments."

1539.   The Association of German Cinema consider this to be the most important German film ever.

1540.   This was Lang's first film with sound.

Mad Max: Fury Road
(2015)

1541. Immorton Joe's mask has horse teeth.

1542. The film took 120 days to shoot. It took nearly four years to edit.

1543. Most of it was shot in the Namibian desert.

1544. Iota played the flame-guitarist, The Doof Warrior. His guitar weighed 132lbs and actually spewed flames.

1545. Despite the violence and gore, the film has almost no profanity. At one point, Max is called a "smeg." "Smeg" was a generic insult used in the television show, Red Dwarf, that was used as a substitute for swearing.

1546. The night scenes were shot in daylight. The colour was altered to make it appear like it was night time.

1547. The film was so complicated that the storyboards were completed before the script.

1548. The storyboards were composed of 3,500 panels.

1549. Nicholas Hoult (who plays Nux) learned how to knit for the film. It took him seven months.

1550. There were only a few dozen actors in the crowd scene. The actors were digitally duplicated so it looked like there were thousands of people.

1551. The last stunt in the film when the War Rig flips was the most dangerous stunt. The director, George Miller, didn't see how it could be done without using CGI. However, the stuntman, Lee Adamson, believed he could do it. When he did it, Miller was certain that he was killed. Luckily, Adamson accomplished the shot on the first take.

1552.   Tom Hardy's stunt double was Dane Grant. Charlize Theron's stunt double was Dayana Porter. Dane said, "we fell in love while we were punching each other." They got married and had a boy.

1553.   80% of the effects are practical.

1554.   Charlize Theron didn't get on with Tom Hardy because of his Method acting.

1555.   The film was shot in sequence.

1556.   The action scenes were so complex, Miller worried that the audience wouldn't know what was going on. To avoid this, he put Max in the centre of almost every shot so the audience wouldn't have to waste time looking for him.

1557.   The villain is played by Hugh Keays-Byrne. He played the villain, Toecutter, in the original Mad Max.

1558.   Charlize Theron broke Tom Hardy's nose during the fights.

1559.   The director, George Miller, hates how apocalyptic films always look dark and murky. He wanted his futuristic dystopia to look bright and beautiful.

1560.   Immorton Joe's has two sons; the simple giant, Rictus Erectus, and the shrivelled but intellectual dwarf, Corpus Colossus. Miller liked the idea of "a child trapped in a man's body and a man trapped in a child's body."

The Magnificent Seven
(1960)

1561. This film was heavily inspired by Seven Samurai.

1562. Anthony Quinn was supposed to play the lead.

1563. Clark Gable was considered for a role.

1564. This film has three sequels.

1565. Steve McQueen and Yul Brynner hated each other during the shoot but made up on McQueen's deathbed.

1566. Yul Brynner was slightly taller than Steve McQueen. However, Brynner wanted to tower over McQueen so he would stand on a little mound when they were in shot together.

1567. Brynner was so certain that McQueen was trying to upstage him that he hired an assistant to count how many times McQueen touched his hat every time Brynner spoke.

1568. Yul Brynner was the only one to come back for the sequel, Return of the Seven.

1569. Brynner was responsible for casting Steve McQueen. He could've removed McQueen from the job once he realised how difficult he was to work with. However, he decided not to, knowing that McQueen was the perfect actor for the role of Vin Tanner.

1570. John Williams played a piano player in this film. He went on to become the greatest music composer in film history. He famously created the theme song for Star Wars.

The Maltese Falcon
(1941)

1571.   Most of the film was shot over Humphrey Bogart's shoulder so the audience will be watching the events of the story from the main character's perspective.

1572.   The seven-minute shot was innovative in its day. It took two days to rehearse.

1573.   Although the history of the Maltese Falcon is extremely detailed and complex, none of it is true.

1574.   Gutman and Wilmer are known as Fat Man and Little Boy. These were the nicknames of the atomic bombs that were dropped on Nagasaki and Hiroshima during World War II.

1575.   The dialogue is identical to the novel it's based off.

1576.   The film was nearly called "The Gent from Frisco."

1577.   Peter Lorre famously plays the character, Cairo. His face was so striking that it was parodied in other films and cartoons. A mad scientist that bears Cairo's resemblance has appeared in many Looney Tunes cartoons. He is usually an antagonist to Daffy Duck and Bugs Bunny.

1578.   This is the film that Peter Lorre is proudest of.

1579.   This was the first film directed by John Huston.

1580.   Three of the Maltese Falcon statuettes still exist and are worth over $1 million each. They are the most expensive film props ever. Each of them are worth three times more than what the film made.

The Matrix
(1999)

1581.   The directors, Larry and Andy Wachowski, considered Tom Cruise, Leonardo DiCaprio, Brad Pitt, Val Kilmer, Johnny Depp, David Duchovny, Will Smith and Ewan McGregor for the part of Neo.

1582.   Nicholas Cage would've accepted the role of Neo except he had family commitments.

1583.   Christopher Walken, Samuel L. Jackson, Gary Oldman, Sean Connery and Tommy Lee Jones were considered for Morpheus.

1584.   Hugo Weaving's monotonous tone for his character, Agent Smith, was based off a boring weatherman Hugo listened to on television.

1585.   Laurence Fishburne wanted Morpheus to have an orange Mohawk.

1586.   Keanu Reeves and Laurence Fishburne assumed they would need a few weeks of training for the fighting scenes. It took five months.

1587.   The Wachowskis went to Warner studio with the idea for The Matrix and asked for $80 million. The studio said that they could only give the directors $10 million. With that money, they did the opening shot of Carrie-Anne Moss' character, Trinity performing the famous Bullet-Time kick. When they showed the shot to Warner Bros. they were blown away and gave them the rest of the money.

1588.   The Bullet-Time effect is accomplished by using 120 cameras surrounding a room, each of which takes a single shot of the room at a specific time, and combining all of the 120 shots together in a seamless action.

1589.   Despite the fact this film is famous for popularising Bullet-Time, the special effect is only used four times –
i)   At the beginning
ii)   When Neo dodges the Agent's bullets
iii)   When Morpheus jumps onto the helicopter
iv)   When Neo fights Agent Smith

1590.   The fighting scenes were choreographed by Woo-Ping Yuen. He is considered to be the greatest fight choreographer in film history. He refused to take part in The Matrix at first because he thought Hollywood fights had too much choppy editing. His technique is to find the best possible angle and show the entire shot from that one angle. He only agreed to work on the film if he had complete control of the choreography. The Wachowskis complied.

1591.   The Wachowskis worked on the concept of the movie for five and a half years and worked through fourteen drafts.

1592.   Some people assumed that the real world scenes are tinted in blue. They aren't. The colour blue stands out more in the real world scenes because it was digitally removed from every Matrix scene.

1593.   The movie had 500 storyboards. Most storyboards look very basic and are only there to give the crew a vague idea what they want to accomplish in a scene. However, the Wachowskis storyboards were incredibly detailed and looked like comic book panels. Speaking of comic books.....

1594.   Many comic book readers have accused The Matrix of stealing the story from the graphic novel, The Invisibles. The Invisibles is about a man who learns that he is the Messiah who lives inside a fake world and he can bend the rules of reality. He learns from a bald, spectacled mentor that the world is secretly controlled by demon insects. (That's the only part that is different.)

Not only is the story suspiciously similar but some of the panels are identical to shots in the film. In The Invisibles Vol. 1 #18, a demon takes the form of an Agent and tries to find vital information in the brain of the Messiah's mentor.

Although the Wachowskis deny this, Grant Morrison, the writer of The Invisibles, has said that he "was told by people on the set that Invisibles books were passed around" on set. So what does he think? Well, he liked the first film. A lot. But when he saw the sequels, he said, "They should have kept on stealing from me."

1595.   The three Agents in the film are called Smith, Jones and Brown.

1596.   Will Smith wanted to do The Matrix but at the last minute, he decided to do Wild Wild West.

1597.   The Wachowskis said that if Keanu Reeves said no to the role, the film wouldn't have been made.

1598.   Keanu Reeves had neck surgery just before starting his training. You can see him wearing a neck brace in clips on the DVD extras.

1599.   All of the scenes in the Matrix are tinted in green. The scenes in the Training Program are tinted in yellow.

1600.   This film came out in 1999. Within three years, the Bullet-Time special effect had been parodied in twenty different films. The first film to parody it was Deuce Bigelow: Male Gigolo.

1601.   Although Bullet-Time looks incredible, it is an incredibly basic technique – still photography. It just requires a lot of preparation... and 120 cameras.

1602.   Despite what many people would believe, this is the only Matrix film that has Bullet-Time special effects. The other films use a completely different special effect called virtual cinematography, which is a 360-degree camera created in a computer.

1603.   The opening action scene took six months of training and four days to shoot.

1604.   Soon after shooting began, Carrie-Anne Moss twisted her ankle. She didn't tell anybody in case she was re-cast.

1605.   Morpheus' ship is called the Nebuchadnezzar. King Nebuchadnezzar was a Biblical king who had a dream he couldn't remember but kept trying to. Morpheus was the Greek god of the dream world.

1606.   In the Women in Red Program, many of the actors were identical twins.

1607.   Hugo Weaving was nearly recast on the first day after a polyp was found on his leg which required surgery.

1608.   The Wachowskis have said that if they were given a choice between the Red Pill or the Blue Pill, they would choose the Blue Pill.

1609.   Apart from Neo's final speech, he never says more than five sentences in a row.

1610.   The scene where Neo climbs up the window was done without a stuntman. Keanu Reeves was standing thirty-four stories high.

Memento
(2000)

1611.   The director, Christopher Nolan, wanted the audience to be as confused as the main character, Leonard. Nolan realised that the only way to do this was show the story in reverse-chronological order. The first scene is the last part of Leonard's story. The film works backwards from that.

1612.   Leonard's amnesia is called Anterograde Amnesia. It is a real disorder that prevents a person to generate new memories due to damage within the hippocampus section of the brain. It tends to happen when parts of the temporal lobe are removed from the brain to treat epilepsy.

1613.   Guy Pearce plays Leonard. It was his idea for Leonard to have bleached hair. Since Leonard can't produce new memories, the only way for him to have a sense of time is to see how much bleach is still in his hair.

1614.   Stephen Tobolowsky, who plays Sammy Jankis, has personally suffered amnesia.

1615.   Alec Baldwin was considered for the part of Leonard.

1616.   Angelina Jolie was considered for Natalie. The role went to Carrie-Anne Moss.

1617.   The film was shot in twenty-five days.

1618.   Carrie-Anne Moss shot her scenes in eight days.

1619.   The film can be watched in chronological order on the DVD.

1620.   SPOILER – When Natalie sees the picture of Leonard pointing to his own chest, he says that spot is reserved for when he finds the killer. At the end of the film, a flashback for a split-second shows Leonard in bed with his wife. The bare spot on his chest says, "I've done it."

Metropolis
(1927)

1621.   The film had 37,000 extras. They were made up of 25,000 men, 11,000 women, 1,100 bald men, 750 children, 100 black people and twenty-five Asians.

1622.   The film was shot in 310 days.

1623.   Lang needed 500 malnourished children for certain scenes. This was very easy since Germany was in financial ruin at the time.

1624.   When Brigitte Helm wore the robot costume for Maria, she fainted because her outfit was so heavy.

1625.   The film was based off the novel of the same name by Thea von Harbou. The novel was heavily inspired by the stories of H.G. Wells. Ironically, Wells hated Metropolis and called it "the silliest film."

1626.   Most of the actors had little to no acting experience.

1627.   The director demanded that extras launch themselves at the jets of water during the flooding scenes.

1628.   Lang would do many takes. It would take up to two days to do the simplest scenes.

1629.   Christopher Nolan watched this film regularly before shooting The Dark Knight Rises.

1630.   Superman writers, Jerry Siegel and Joe Shuster, loved the film so much that they named Superman's home city after the film's title.

Midnight Cowboy
(1969)

1631. The famous line "I'm walking here!" was an accident. Dustin Hoffman nearly got hit by a car and he ad-libbed the line.

1632. This is the first X-rated film to win the Best Picture Oscar.

1633. Dustin Hoffman was told by his agent that his career would be destroyed if he starred in this film.

1634. Hoffman kept pebbles in his shoes to make his limp look genuine.

1635. Hoffman got so into the character during the scene where Ratso has a coughing fit, that he actually vomited.

1636. Warren Beatty was meant to play Buck but the studio thought he was too famous and he would be distracting in the role.

1637. This was the first film to use the word "scuzzy."

1638. Harrison Ford auditioned for the lead.

1639. Jon Voight struggled so much with the Texan accent that he was nearly fired.

1640. Elvis Presley was very interested in the lead role.

Million Dollar Baby
(2004)

1641.   Clint Eastwood directed the film. He is the oldest person to win the Best Director Oscar. He was seventy-four.

1642.   Clint Eastwood's ninety-six-year-old mother was in the audience when he won the Oscar.

1643.   Clint Eastwood wanted Morgan Freeman to play the lead role.

1644.   Hilary Swank gained 20lbs of muscle for the part.

1645.   Many Irish people complained that the Gaelic language that Clint's character, Frankie, speaks is completely wrong. However, Irish people don't speak Gaelic now; they speak Gaeilge. Even modern Irish people get the two languages confused because the languages are similar but not identical. The Gaelic that Frankie speaks is accurate.

1646.   Frankie says that "mo chuisle" means "my darling" or "my love." Its direct translation is "my pulse." It comes from the Gaelic phrase "a chuisle mo chroi," which means "pulse of my heart."

1647.   Sandra Bullock was supposed to play Maggie.

1648.   The film was completed two days early.

1649.   Hilary Swank has said that her character was very similar to how she was brought up.

1650.   The film four Oscars. It won more Oscars than any other sports film.

Modern Times
(1936)

1651. Charlie Chaplin's character is called A Factory Worker.

1652. Chaplin said he was inspired to make this film after he spoke to Gandhi. He told Chaplin that society have become over-reliant on machines.

1653. The film was going to be called "The Masses."

1654. John Lithgow said this is his favourite film.

1655. Modern Times is considered to be the best film Chaplin ever made.

1656. This is considered to be the greatest silent film ever.

1657. Although it is considered to be a silent film, there are some sounds including the radio, the videophones and the Mechanical Salesman.

1658. This was meant to be Chaplin's first sound film.

1659. Dialogue was written for the entire film but it was thrown out at the last minute.

1660. This is considered to be the final film of the Silent Era.

Monty Python and the Holy Grail
(1975)

1661.   The movie's tagline was, "Makes Ben-Hur look like an epic."

1662.   Another tagline was, "Funnier than Psycho and shorter than Ben-Hur."

1663.   Connie Booth plays the witch at the beginning of the film. She became John Cleese's wife.

1664.   Michael Palin played twelve characters.

1665.   In Japan, the film is called "Holy Sake Cup."

1666.   This is considered to be Monty Python's greatest film.

1667.   This is often considered to be Britain's funniest film.

1668.   Instead of soldiers galloping on horses, soldiers were followed by an associate who taps coconut-shells to make the sound effect of a horse trotting. This was done because the film's budget was so tight, that they couldn't afford horses.

1669.   A real rabbit was used for the Killer Rabbit scene. He was dyed with a red liquid for some shots. The rabbit's owner was very sad to learn that the red liquid wouldn't wash off the rabbit. Ever.

1670.   All of the armour is made of wool.

1671.   The image for God was actually a 19th century English cricketer called W.G. Grace.

1672.   The Bridge Keeper asks the question, "What is the capital of Assyria?" The correct answer is Assur.

1673.   The Bridge Keeper asks the question, "What is airspeed velocity of an unladen swallow?" The correct answer is 24mph.

1674.   Graham Chapman played the lead part, King Arthur. He suffered horrific alcoholism throughout filming.

1675.   Graham Chapman was the only person who wore real chain mail. It weighed 25lbs.

1676.   The budget was so low, that most of the extras were played by the crew.

1677.   John Cleese played Tim the Enchanter. He chose the name because he forgot the character's actual name on the first take when he said, "There are some who call me......... Tim."

1678.   Michael Palin stood on a ladder to play the chief Knight-who-says-"Ni."

1679.   All of the female parts are played by women. This is rare for a Monty Python film.

1680.   The reason why the film ends so abruptly is because they ran out of money.

Mr. Smith Goes to Washington
(1939)

1681.   The film was banned in many countries in Europe, including Italy, France, Russia, Spain and Germany.

1682.   Some countries that showed the film changed the subtitles so it would not talk about political corruption as much.

1683.   American politicians were furious that the film suggested that Washington was corrupt.

1684.   The director, Frank Capra, said that he has received many letters from people who watched the film and were inspired to go into politics.

1685.   James Stewart knew this film would make his career. He was so worried that something might happen to hit him before he became a Hollywood star that he would drive to the studio at a snail's pace, worried that he would be hit by a car.

1686.   Beulah Bondi played Mr. Smith's mother. This is one of five films where Bondi has played James Stewart's mother.

1687.   Senators were known to talk out in disgust in the middle of the film.

1688.   The lead actress, Jean Arthur, didn't like working with James Stewart. She didn't think he was a strong actor.

1689.   Capra had to reference the Boy Scouts at one point. However, the Boy Scouts refused to have anything to do with the film. As a result, Capra had to reference the fictitious group, The Boy Rangers.

1690.   The Washington Press intentionally gave it bad reviews after they were portrayed in a negative light.

Nausicaa of the Valley of the Wind
(1984)

1691.   This film was released in 1984. Shia LeBeouf (who was born in 1986) plays Asbel in the English dub. This means that Shia is credited for the film even though he wasn't born until after the film was originally released.

1692.   The film was heavily re-edited and released worldwide in 1985 as "Warriors of the Wind." The original director, Hayao Miyazaki, hated it.

1693.   Miyazaki was so upset about the Western version of this film that when a producer said he wanted to edit Miyazaki's film, Princess Mononoke, Miyazaki sent him a sword with the words, "NO CUTS" written on it.

1694.   The English dub has an amazing cast including Mark Hamill, Patrick Stewart, Tony Jay, Uma Thurman, Frank Welker and Edward James Olmos.

1695.   Because it was directed by Miyazaki, many fans assume that this a Studio Ghibli film. However, the film was made before Studio Ghibli was formed.

1696.   Miyazaki was worried the film wouldn't sell because it wasn't based off any book or merchandise. To counter this, he created a comic based off the story to promote the film.

1697.   The military planes are based off the Nazi Luftwaffe.

1698.   The female is called Obaba. Her name means "great old woman."

1699.   Nausicaa's glider is called Mehve. "Mehve" is German for "seagull."

1700.   The name "Nausicaa" comes from a character in Homer's Odyssey.

Network
(1976)

1701.   Beatrice Straight was on screen for five minutes and two seconds and won an Oscar. It is the shortest performance to ever win an Oscar.

1702.   Some people believe that the film is intentionally over-the-top because it is a satire. However, the director and screenwriter said that how they depicted how television networks think very accurately.

1703.   James Stewart turned down a role.

1704.   This is the last film to receive five Oscar nominations in acting categories.

1705.   All of the music from the film is from commercials and tv theme songs.

1706.   Henry Fonda was considered for a role.

1707.   This was the last film Peter Finch ever worked on.

1708.   Sidney Lumet was furious that the film lost the Best Picture Oscar to Rocky.

1709.   Although this film is considered to be the debut of Tim Robbins, he's not in the film.

1710.   Ned Beatty got an Oscar nomination for his role. He worked on the film for one day.

The Nightmare Before Christmas
(1994)

1711. If you look closely at the film's opening, you will see that the bats are on wires. This movie is stop-motioned so the wires are completely unnecessary. They were put in as a reference to the awful special effects from old horror movies (especially the bats in the film, Dracula.)

1712. Danny Elfman created ten songs for the film. He said this film was the easiest job he ever had.

1713. Zero's nose is a small jack-o-lantern.

1714. Vincent Price was supposed to play Santa Claus.

1715. Every second of the film required twelve stop-motion moves.

1716. A hundred people took three years to complete this film.

1717. Patrick Stewart was supposed to be the narrator.

1718. The story began as a three-page poem by Tim Burton when he was an animator for Disney in the 1980s.

1719. Tim Burton couldn't direct the film as he was busy making Ed Wood.

1720. Danny Elfman provides the singing for the lead, Jack Skellington.

No Country for Old Men
(2007)

1721.   The villain's name, Anton Chigurh, is supposed to sound foreign but it's not clear what country it is based from. The writer, Cormac McCarthy did this so the name didn't sound like it came from a specific country.

1722.   When Javier Bardem saw the hairstyle he was going to have for his character, he said, "No girl is going to go near me for months!"

1723.   Chigurh's silencer is a fictional weapon.

1724.   Javier Bardem is a Method actor. This was the first film where he didn't use the Method because he couldn't believe that a human being could be as evil as Chigurh.

1725.   When Bardem was offered the part, he said, "I don't drive, I speak bad English, and I hate violence." The directors say, "That's why we called you."

1726.   Josh Brolin broke his shoulder two days before winning the part and he was terrified he would be recast. Luckily, his injury didn't become an issue as his character is shot in the shoulder early in the film.

1727.   Heath Ledger was considered for the lead part.

1728.   Javier Bardem won an Oscar for this film. He is the first Spanish actor to win an Oscar.

1729.   The title comes from W.B. Yeats poem, "Sailing to Byzantium." The first line is "That is no country for old men."

1730.   No Country for Old Men has one of the weirdest coincidences in film history. The sheriff says that the dope-dealers "killed a federal judge." They killed the judge in San Antonio in 1980. This was based off a real judge who was killed in 1979 in San Antonio by a contract killer called Charles Harrelson. This contract killer is the father of Woody Harrelson... who also happens to be in the film!

North by Northwest
(1959)

1731.   Cary Grant played the lead role. The director, Alfred Hitchcock, always wanted Grant to play the role. This posed a problem as James Stewart had just worked on Vertigo with Hitchcock and he assumed he was going to play the lead in this film. Hitchcock didn't want to hurt his feelings so he waited until Stewart was working on another film. He then offered Stewart the role, knowing that he wouldn't be able to take it.

1732.   In one scene, Cary Grant's character, Roger, is in a car with with a cop. The cop forgets to lean to give the illusion that the car is turning. You can see Cary Grant angrily poking the other actor to remind him he is supposed to lean.

1733.   Roger is on the left of almost every scene in the film.

1734.   Hitchcock said that he was so happy with how the film turned out that he only had to remove five seconds from the first cut for the final cut.

1735.   The Production Code had a problem with Martin Landau's performance because they found him too camp. They said this sort of behaviour was inappropriate for the film.

1736.   Gregory Peck was strongly considered for the lead role.

1737.   Elizabeth Taylor was considered for the part of Eve.

1738.   Yul Brynner was considered for the part of Vandamm.

1739.   Hitchcock plays the man in the beginning who misses the bus.

1740.   This film has a famous mistake. In the diner scene, Eve fires a gun. A boy extra in the background knows it's about to happen sticks his fingers in his ears to prepare for the loud bang.

On the Waterfront
(1954)

1741.   Marlon Brando wasn't sure if he wanted to play the lead of Terry Malloy. To encourage Brando to take the part, the director, Elia Kazan, offered the part to a young pretty actor who just finished acting school. Brando was very competitive so when he heard of this other actor, he instantly accepted the role. The other actor was Paul Newman.

1742.   Frank Sinatra was considered for the lead role.

1743.   Montgomery Clift was considered for a part.

1744.   Arthur Miller wrote the script but it was rejected.

1745.   Most of the shoot occurred near Mafia hangouts.

1746.   Although Brando's performance in this film is considered to be one of the greatest acting performances ever, Brando thought it was his worst performance. When he first saw the film, he considered himself to be a failure.

1747.   The original title was going to be "Bottom of the River."

1748.   Brando won an Oscar for the role but he lost it soon after.

1749.   While Marlon Brando and Eve Marie Saint were rehearsing the park scene, Saint dropped her glove. Most actors would stop the scene and start again. However, Brando had a tendency to continue scenes even after mistakes happened. After Saint dropped the glove, Brando picked it up and put it on. Kazan liked this because he thought Terry would react this way to taunt Saint's character. They kept the glove-wearing scene in the finished film.

1750.   Marlon Brando was only able to work until 4pm because he had sessions with his counsellor. His mother died just before the film and he needed to deal with many unresolved issues with his parents.

Once Upon a Time in America
(1984)

1751. When the filming was complete, the footage ran nearly ten hours.

1752. The director, Sergio Leone, struggled cutting the film down. Originally, he cut it down to six hours and thought he couldn't cut it anymore so he had no choice but to released it as two films. The produced rejected this idea so he had to cut it down to 229 minutes.

1753. Although the official version of the film is the 229-minute version, the producers cut the film down to 144 minutes. This was the version that was released in cinemas. So much was cut out, that it was considered incomprehensible, made little money, was torn apart by critics and received no nominations.

1754. This was Jennifer Connelly's film debut.

1755. Sergio Leone turned down the opportunity to direct The Godfather and always regretted it. He eventually decided to make his own gangster epic with this film.

1756. Leone borrowed a lot of themes from The Godfather films, especially the flashback techniques from The Godfather: Part II.

1757. Al Pacino was considered for the lead role.

1758. John Belushi was supposed to play Max but he suddenly died.

1759. Jack Nicholson turned down the lead role.

1760.   James Woods said that a critic saw the 144-minute version and said it was the worst film of 1984. That same critic saw the 229-minute version years later and said it was one of the best films of that 1980s.

Once Upon a Time in the West
(1968)

1761.   Sergio Leone cast Henry Fonda as the lead villain. Fonda was known for only playing good guys so Leone wanted to shock the audience when the villain was revealed in the opening scene.

1762.   Fonda was not used to playing a villain so he wore brown contact lenses and grew a moustache. When Leone saw him, he told him to get rid of his lenses and facial hair. He said that the only way to shock the audience was for them to see Fonda they way they knew him rather than him "trying to play a villain."

1763.   In the opening scene, a fly lands on the cheek of the actor, Jack Elam. The filmmakers accomplished this by putting jam on his face.

1764.   Clint Eastwood turned down a part.

1765.   High Noon heavily inspired Leone while making this film.

1766.   One of the stuntmen was John Landis, the director of Animal House, The Twilight Zone, An American Werewolf in London and Coming to America.

1767.   Kirk Douglas auditioned for a part.

1768.   Terence Stamp was considered for Harmonica.

1769.   Warren Beatty auditioned for Harmonica.

1770.   One of the actors, Al Mulock, committed suicide. He jumped out of a hotel window while he was wearing his costume. When his body was being put in a car to be driven to a hospital, Leone screamed, "Get the costume! We need the costume!"

What a guy.

One Flew Over the Cuckoo's Nest
(1975)

1771.   This is the film debut of Christopher Lloyd and Brad Dourif.

1772.   This was one of the first films Danny DeVito, Vincent Schiavelli and Michael Berryman ever did.

1773.   Many of the extras were mental patients.

1774.   Jack Nicholson didn't think he was very good while he was filming. He was intimidated by how professional the extras were as they seemed to be staying in character 24/7. He had no idea they were actually mentally ill.

1775.   Kirk Douglas bought the rights for this film so he could star as the lead character, McMurphy. However, by the time the film was ready to shoot, he was too old.

1776.   The film was kick-started by Kirk Douglas' son, Michael Douglas. He was the producer.

1777.   Louise Fletcher played the callous Nurse Ratchett. She hated how cold she had to be on set while everyone else was enjoying herself.

1778.   This film is based off Ken Kesey's novel of the same title. He absolutely detested the film.

1779.   In the novel, McMurphy was a huge, red-haired Irishman.

1780.   Will Sampson played the Chief. This was his film debut.

1781.   Will Sampson was 6ft 5.

1782.   The Chief was very hard to cast as it was almost impossible to find giant Native Americans.

1783.   Marlon Brando turned down the lead role.

1784.   Burt Reynolds was considered for the role of McMurphy.

1785.   Danny DeVito was the first to be cast.

1786.   The story is based off Ken Kesey's experience as a guard at a mental hospital.

1787.   A lot of Jack Nicholson's dialogue is improvised, especially his first few scenes.

1788.   The film was so successful in Sweden that it was shown in cinemas for twelve years straight.

1789.   Every actor had to spend time with at least two different mental patients to see how they acted.

1790.   By a complete coincidence, Jack Nicholson, Danny DeVito and Vincent Schiavelli have all played Batman villains.

Pan's Labyrinth
(2006)

1791.   The director, Guillermo del Toro, said this film is "a womb with a view." I don't know what that means.

1792.   Pan and the Pale Man are played by the same actor, Doug Jones. Doug has worked on almost every film that del Toro has directed.

1793.   Doug Jones tends to get cast as bizarre creatures like Pan or the Pale Man because he is so skinny, that he fits into his costumes like a second skin. Del Toro has said that if an ordinary sized man were to wear the same costume, he just looks like "some guy wearing a costume."

1794.   Del Toro did the English subtitles himself.

1795.   When the film ended at the Cannes Film Festival, it received a twenty-two-minute applause.

1796.   It took five hours for Doug Jones to get into the Pale Man costume.

1797.   Because the Pale Man has no eyes on his face, Jones could only see through the nostrils.

1798.   Doug Jones was the only American on set. He was also the only person who couldn't speak Spanish.

1799.   Del Toro turned down the offer to direct The Lion, the Witch and the Wardrobe to make this film.

1800.   Guillermo del Toro was offered double the budget if he made the film in English. He said no.

Papillon
(1973)

1801.   Roman Polanski was supposed to direct this film.

1802.   Warren Beatty was meant to play the lead role.

1803.   Dustin Hoffman had to wear contact lenses so he could see through his thick glasses.

1804.   The actors and crew were heavily intoxicated with marijuana throughout the shoot.

1805.   This was written by Dalton Trumbo. He was uncredited because he was a member of the Communist Party.

1806.   Hoffman based his character off the writer, Trumbo.

1807.   Dustin Hoffman and Steve McQueen hated working together.

1808.   McQueen refused to use a stuntman for the cliff scene and he demanded that he would jump off the cliff himself. He said it was "one of the most exhilarating experiences of my life."

1809.   Papillon is considered to be the last great Steve McQueen film.

1810.   Although this is considered a true story, most of the events that happen to Papillon are fictitious. He never served any time on the Devil Islands.

Paths of Glory
(1957)

1811.   The title comes from the saying, "The paths of glory lead but to the grave."

1812.   Kirk Douglas agreed to make the film, believing that it wouldn't make any money. Sadly, he was right.

1813.   The director, Stanley Kubrick, met his third wife, Christiane, during this film.

1814.   Douglas was paid $350,000 for the film.

1815.   It was banned in Spain, Franch and Sweden for up to twenty-nine years for being anti-military.

1816.   The film was shot in Munich. Most of the French soldiers are actually Munich police officers.

1817.   Gregory Peck was supposed to play the lead but he was busy.

1818.   Kubrick had to create "dying zones" for each actor, who had to memorize the exact spot on the battleground where they were supposed to fall down dead.

1819.   Kubrick had to make the trenches wider than the real trenches of WWII so his cameras could fit in them.

1820.   Winston Churchill said the film was astonishingly accurate with how it depicted trench warfare as well as the miscommunication from the military.

Patton
(1970)

1821.   Friends of the real Patton said George C. Scott's performance was perfect apart from the fact that Patton cursed a lot more.

1822.   This is one of Richard Nixon's favourite films.

1823.   The opening speech is compiled of many quotes that Patton actually said.

1824.   Francis Ford Coppola wrote a draft for the film in 1966. He was fired for it.

1825.   George C. Scott regularly apologised to the director for not being good enough to play Patton.

1826.   Scott refused his Oscar, claiming that the award ceremony was a "meat parade."

1827.   John Huston was considered for the director's chair.

1828.   Robert Mitchum turned down the lead role.

1829.   This was the first PG film to win Best Picture.

1830.   Scott wanted the beginning monologue to be at the very end. He believed it was written so well that if he started the film with it, the rest of the story wouldn't be able to top it.

The Pianist
(2002)

1831.   When Adrien Brody won the lead role, he wanted to experience what it was like to lose everything like his character. As a result, he dumped his long-term partner and sold most of his possessions, stopped watching television and got rid of his apartment.

1832.   Adrien Brody won an Oscar for this film when he was twenty-nine. He is the youngest man to ever win the Oscar for Best Actor. It's pretty impressive since he competed against Jack Nicholson (three-time Oscar winner,) Daniel Day-Lewis (three-time Oscar winner) Michael Caine (two-time Oscar winner) and Nicholas Cage (one-time Oscar winner.)

1833.   Brody lost 31lbs for the role.

1834.   All the piano-playing was performed by Brody.

1835.   Joseph Fiennes was supposed to play the lead role.

1836.   Brody plays Wladyslaw Szpilman. Szpilman died while the film was being made.

1837.   The film is an account of Szpilman's life but the director, Roman Polanski, also added in events from his own life during the war.

1838.   This is the first film Polanski made in his home country of Poland in fifty years.

1839.   1,400 actors auditioned for the lead role.

1840.   By a complete coincidence, Polanski was looking for locations for the film, he happened to meet a man who helped Polanski's family survive the war.

Pirates of the Caribbean: The Curse of the Black Pearl
(2003)

1841.   The studio was furious with Johnny Depp during filming as they had no idea what to make of his character.

1842.   Geoffrey Rush likes to stand on the left of his scenes, believing that the audience naturally look at images in the film from left-to-right like the way a person reads a book. If he stands on the left, Rush believes that the audience will always see him first.

1843.   The monkey is called Jack.

1844.   Will Turner is supposed to be the best swordsman, then Barbossa, then Jack Sparrow.

1845.   Johnny Depp wanted Jack Sparrow to have phobias of peppers and colds.

1846.   Robert De Niro was offered the role of Jack Sparrow.

1847.   Keira Knightley was so convinced she was going to get fired that she barely packed anything.

1848.   Johnny Depp's contact lenses worked as sunglasses because he didn't want to squint for the whole film.

1849.   Heath Ledger nearly played Will Turner.

1850.   Johnny Depp wanted Jack Sparrow to have no nose.

Planet of the Apes
(1968)

1851. The actors couldn't take off their masks in-between takes. As a result, their lunch and dinner was liquefied and fed to them with a straw.

1852. This is one of the first films to have a toy-merchandise tie-in.

1853. The ape-actors had to eat their food in front of a mirror to make sure they didn't alter any of their make-up.

1854. The make-up cost £345,542. It made up 17% of the entire budget.

1855. The film takes place in the year, 3978.

1856. The film is based off the French novel of the same name. It was written by Pierre Boulle. Boulle believed it was the worst novel he ever wrote.

1857. Charlton Heston didn't like the original novel.

1858. The rights for the novel were bought before it was even published.

1859. The concept for the famous ending was taken from the Twilight Zone episode: I Shot an Arrow into the Air. The writer of the original novel hated the ending for the film. He believed his ending was much better. The original ending from the novel was used in the 2011 remake of Planet of the Apes. It is often considered to be the worst twist/ending in film history.

1860. In between shots, the same ape species ate together; orang-utans with orang-utans, chimps with chimps and gorillas with gorillas. Nobody decided this. It just happened instinctively.

Platoon
(1986)

1861.   The director, Oliver Stone, is the first person to serve in Vietnam to direct a film about the Vietnam War.

1862.   Charlie Sheen played the lead role, Chris. However, the part was meant to be played by his brother, Emilio Estevez.

1863.   Mickey Rourke turned down the part of Sgt. Barnes.

1864.   Kris Kristofferson was considered for the part of Elias.

1865.   This is considered to be the first of Stone's Vietnam trilogy. The other films are Heaven and Earth and Born on the Fourth of July.

1866.   James Woods turned down a role in the film because "he couldn't take the mud."

1867.   Oliver Stone has a cameo as the bunker officer who gets blown up by a suicide runner.

1868.   Most of the film was shot sequentially.

1869.   This film is banned in Vietnam.

1870.   The film made Stone relive a lot of moments he experienced in Vietnam, which made him suffer Post-Traumatic Stress Disorder.

The Prestige
(2006)

1871. The writer of the book this film is based off said that he wished he started the story with the same dialogue Michael Caine says in the introduction.

1872. The word "prestige" comes from the Latin word, "praestigium," which means "illusion."

1873. Borden's son is played by Christopher Nolan's son.

1874. Andy Serkis' character makes a reference to guessing what is in a person's pocket. This is a reference to how his character, Gollum, was tricked in the book, The Hobbit.

1875. Scarlet Johansson and Rebecca Hall star in this film. Weirdly, they both starred in Vicky Cristina Barcelona.

1876. Hugh Jackman and Andy Serkis star in this film. They also starred in Flushed Away the same year this film came out.

1877. Josh Hartnett was considered for the lead role.

1878. Six of the actors in this film have starred in comic book films.

1879. This film was nearly directed by Sam Mendes.

1880. The "goldfish bowl" magician is based off a real magician called William Ellsworth Robinson (although his stage name was Chung Ling Soo. He died on stage when a bullet catching trick went wrong. Before he died, he said, "My God, I've been shot." It was the only time he spoke English on stage in nineteen years.

The Princess Bride
(1987)

1881.   When Andre the Giant's character, Fezzik, had to hold Buttercup, she was held up by wires because Andre physically couldn't hold her due to his severe back problems.

1882.   Andre the Giant said that his favourite part of the film was how "Nobody looked at me." He said he felt like an equal throughout the shoot.

1883.   Mandy Patinkin said he only suffered one injury and it wasn't from any of the fights or stunts. He injured a rib because Billy Crystal kept making him laugh.

1884.   Arnold Schwarzenegger was strongly considered for the role of Fezzik.

1885.   The director, Rob Reiner, couldn't be on set during Billy Crystal's scenes because he was laughing so much.

1886.   Uma Thurman was nearly cast as Buttercup.

1887.   Christopher Reeve was considered for the lead.

1888.   Danny DeVito was supposed to play the villain, Vizzini.

1889.   Andre didn't know who was who on set so he called everybody "boss."

1890.   Mandy Patinkin famously says the line, "My name is Inigo Montoya. You killed my father. Prepare to die." Patinkin says that people say this to him at least two or three times a day.

Princess Mononoke
(1997)

1891. There are 550 colours in the film.

1892. "Mononoke" means "vengeful spirit."

1893. This was the most expensive anime upon its release.

1894. Leonardo DiCaprio was considered for the part of Ashitaka.

1895. The film was made of 144,000 animation cells.

1896. Of the 144,000 cells, the director personally corrected or redrew 80,000 of them.

1897. In Japanese mythology, dogs and wolves are male-voiced and cats are female-voice. This was integrated into the plot.

1898. This was supposed to be the director's final film. However, it became so successful that he has made several films since.

1899. This is the second longest anime ever. It's 134 minutes long.

1900. It was the last major animated film to be filmed on plastic animation cels.

Prisoners
(2013)

1901.   Loki's story is heavily based off Norse mythology and the mythological character, Loki.

1902.   Mark Wahlberg and Christian Bale were originally supposed to star. They both dropped out to work on The Fighter.

1903.   Bryan Singer was supposed to be the director. Eventually, Dennis Villeneuve took on the directing duties.

1904.   This is Dennis Villeneuve's first film in English.

1905.   Hugh Jackman plays a father who's desperately looking for his presumed-dead daughter. He was supposed to star in The Lovely Bones, where he would play a father who was looking for his presumed-dead daughter. The part went to Mark Wahlberg... who nearly played Hugh Jackman's part in this film!

1906.   Jake Gyllenhaal plays Detective Loki. In the notes he finds at Bob Taylor's, there is a drawing of a rabbit that looks like the rabbit from the film, Donnie Darko. Jake Gyllenhaal played the lead in that film.

1907.   Leonard DiCaprio was considered for the lead.

1908.   Villeneuve loved working with Gyllenhaal so much that he said that he wanted to work with him in his next film. Their next film together was Enemy.

1909.   Jessica Chastain was considered for a role.

1910.   Detective Loki wears a Freemason ring.

Psycho
(1960)

1911.   It was filmed in thirty days.

1912.   Although many people consider Hitchcock a "horror director," this was his first horror film. He only made one other horror film; The Birds.

1913.   None of the crew or actors knew the ending until Hitchcock had to shoot it.

1914.   The killer was heavily inspired by real-life murderer, Ed Gein.

1915.   On the first day, the cast and crew had to raise their hand and make a sworn oath they would not divulge any of the film's details.

1916.   The blood in the shower scene was made from chocolate syrup.

1917.   This was the last black-and-white film Hitchcock directed.

1918.   In the shower scene, the knife is never seen stabbing Marion.

1919.   The stabbing in the shower scene was done by Hitchcock himself.

1920.   SPOILER – In its time, it was very shocking to see the lead character be killed off halfway through the film.

Pulp Fiction
(1994)

1921. When the director, Quentin Tarantino, first suggested John Travolta for the part of Vincent Vega, the other writers burst out laughing because they thought he was joking.

1922. Uma Thurman wasn't interested in the film. Tarantino was so desperate for her to star in the film that he read the script with her on the phone.

1923. The passage that Jules quotes from the Bible is fictitious.

1924. Although it is never said in the film, the mysterious briefcase contains diamonds. Tarantino's previous film, Reservoir Dogs, revolves around stolen diamonds and he didn't want to do the same thing in this film so he never directly mentions them.

1925. Pulp Fiction is ranked #7 on the top 250 greatest films on IMDB.

1926. Marsellus Wallace has a bandage on the back of his neck because the actor, Ving Rhames, has a scar there.

1927. Christopher Walken played Captain Koons. Tarantino rang him once to make sure he was still available for shooting his scene. Walken didn't answer. As the day came closer, Tarantino started to worry as he was unable to contact Walken. On the day of Koons' scene, everything was set up even though Tarantino was unsure if Walken would show up. Walken came in on time, did his scene in one take and then left.

1928.   Tarantino nearly played the part of Lance (the guy who tells everybody what to do in the overdosing scene.)

1929.   Jules' wallet belongs to Tarantino.

1930.   Jules' wallet is a reference to the lyrics to the Shaft theme song.

1931.   Uma Thurman HATES the song she had to dance to.

1932.   Vincent Vega was written for Michael Madsen.

1933.   Daniel Day-Lewis really wanted to play Vincent.

1934.   Pam Grier auditioned for the part of Lance's wife, Jody. She went on to play the title character in Tarantino's film, Jackie Brown.

1935.   Jules was supposed to have an afro. Instead he had a jheri curl wig.

1936.   The famous dance that John Travolta and Uma Thurman is copied move by movement from the dance scene in the film, 8½.

1937.   Michelle Pfeiffer auditioned for Mia.

1938.   The film was nearly called "Black Mask."

1939.   John Travolta's character, Vincent, is the brother of Michael Madsen's character, Vic (Mr. Blonde) in the film, Reservoir Dogs.

1940.   Pumpkin is played by Tim Roth. The part nearly went to Christian Slater.

1941.   Jules was nearly played by Eddie Murphy.

1942.   Charles S. Dutton was considered for Marcellus Wallace.

1943.   Tommy Lee Jones was considered for Captain Koons.

1944.   Tarantino has a habit of using feet a lot in his films. Uma Thurman is barefoot for nearly the entire film. Also, the cab driver, Esmeralda, doesn't wear shoes.

1945.   A light bulb was put in the briefcase to make it glow.

1946.   Something bad happens every time Vincent goes to the bathroom.

1947.   The film cost $8 million. $5 million went to the actor's salaries.

1948.   Bruce Willis worked on the film for eighteen days.

1949.   Vincent is the only person who is in every story.

1950.   The heart-stabbing scene was done backwards and shot in reverse.

Raging Bull
(1980)

1951.   For years, Robert De Niro held the world record for the most weight gained for a film. He gained 60lbs for this role by eating "lots of pasta."

1952.   When the director, Martin Scorsese, saw De Niro after he put on the weight, he shut down production, terrified that De Niro would die.

1953.   The script was written in two weeks.

1954.   De Niro fought in three Brooklyn boxing matches while he was preparing for the film. He won two of them.

1955.   The sound effects from the punches were created by smashing tomatoes and melons.

1956.   Scorsese made the film in black-and-white to differentiate it from Rocky.

1957.   De Niro did a thousand rounds with the real Jake LaMotta.

1958.   There's only ten minutes of boxing in the film.

1959.   It took six weeks to shoot the boxing scenes.

1960.   After De Niro's training, LaMotta believed that he could be a professional boxer.

1961.   The main reason Jake LaMotta had anger problems was because he was nearly deaf and he would snap when he didn't understand what people were saying.

1962.   Martin Scorsese thought this would be his final film as he was extremely ill during production.

1963.   De Niro broke Joe Pesci's rib in the sparring scene. Pesci's reaction has genuine.

1964.   De Niro and Pesci actually punched each other in the "hit me" scenes.

1965.   Chocolate syrup was used for blood in the film. It was exactly the same syrup used for the film, Psycho.

1966.   This was John Turturro's film debut.

1967.   Sharon Stone auditioned for the role of Vicki.

1968.   The wall that De Niro punches and head-butts before he goes to jail was actually made of concrete.

1969.   When Robert De Niro won an Oscar for the film, he said this in his speech, "I would like to thank my parents for having me and my grandparents for having them. I would like to thank Jake LaMotta... and his brother, Joey LaMotta... even though he's suing us. "

1970.   Jake LaMotta asked his wife, Vicki, if he was as bad as he was depicted in the film. She said, "You were worse."

Raiders of the Lost Ark
(1981)

1971.   Alfred Molina plays Satipo in the beginning in one of his first roles.

1972.   The iconic punch sound effects were created by punching a pile of leather jackets with a baseball bat.

1973.   In the Well of Souls, the Star Wars characters, R2-D2 and C-3PO appear on the wall on a golden pillar near the Ark.

1974.   Indiana Jones famously shoots a swordsman instead of fighting him. Harrison Ford did this because he was suffering from diarrhoea. The swordsman was annoyed because he spent weeks choreographing his fight scene.

1975.   Tom Selleck was supposed to play Indiana Jones. His audition tape can be viewed on YouTube.

1976.   Indiana Jones' whip is made of kangaroo hide.

1977.   The whip was sold at an auction for $43,000.

1978.   Indiana never loses his hat.

1979.   Until the first day of production, the lead was going to be called Indiana Smith.

1980.   This was the most successful film of 1981.

1981.   Most of the snakes in the Well of Souls aren't snakes. They are legless lizards. You can tell because they have earholes. Snakes don't.

1982.   Klaus Kinski was offered the role of the villain, Toht.

1983.   Toht's name is never said in the film.

1984.   "Toht" is German for "death."

1985.   Toht was supposed to have a mechanical arm that could turn into a machine gun. He was also meant to have a radio antenna built into his head.

1986.   Danny DeVito was considered for the role of Sallah. The role went to John Rhys-Davies.

1987.   Thirty whips were made for the film.

1988.   Different whips were used for different scenes. The smallest whip was 6ft. The longest whip was 16ft.

1989.   The shoot in Tunisia was supposed to take six weeks but Spielberg did it in less than five weeks because he found the heat unbearable and wanted to get out of there as soon as possible.

1990.   Indiana's hat was designed so the brim would shadow Indiana's eyes. This would obscure Indiana when he was played by stunt doubles.

1991.   The boulder was made of fiberglass.

1992.   This film was supposed to have a super-small budget. It didn't. At all.

1993.   This was the first film Spielberg directed in the UK.

1994.   Jeff Bridges turn down the lead role.

1995.   Pat Roach died twice in this film. He plays a mechanic and a Sherpa.

1996.   In the airplane fight scene, the vehicle ran over Harrison Ford's knee and tore his ligaments. He continued the scene.

1997.   George Lucas didn't want to cast Harrison Ford as Indiana Jones.

1998.   When Belloq opens the Ark, the language he speaks is Aramaic, the same language spoken in Israel at the time of Christ.

1999.   Jonathan Pryce was considered for Belloq.

2000.   The special effects for the spirits at the end were created by shooting mannequins underwater in slow-mo through a blurry lens.

Rain Man
(1988)

2001. In the original script, Raymond was described as "mentally disabled." It was Dustin Hoffman's idea to make the character an autistic savant.

2002. When Hoffman said he wanted to play Raymond as an autistic, the director said, "Why would he be artistic?!!" The director never heard the word "autistic" before.

2003. Hoffman thought his performance was terrible while he was filming. He once told the director, "Get Richard Dreyfuss, this is the worst work of my life." The part won him a Best Acting Oscar.

2004. Originally, Hoffman was cast as Charlie. He told the director that he thought Raymond would be a more interesting character to play. Tom Cruise replaced Hoffman as Charlie.

2005. Jack Nicholson turned down the part of Raymond.

2006. The boy at the pancake counter is Dustin Hoffman's son, Jake.

2007. Robert De Niro was considered for Raymond.

2008. Raymond says that Qantas has never lost a jet airliner. As of today, this is still true.

2009. The line about Qantas never losing a jet was supposed to be made up. The writer didn't realise that it was actually true.

2010. The director, Barry Levinson, played the psychiatrist that decides if Raymond should stay with Charlie.

2011. Hoffman spent a year working with autistic families to prepare for the role.

2012. This was the most successful film of 1988.

2013. This was Princess Diana's favourite film.

2014. The two leads were nearly played by the Quaid brothers, Randy and Dennis.

2015. The scene where Raymond gives airline statistics is usually removed from most inflight viewings of the film.

2016. Bill Murray was considered for the role of Charlie.

2017. Before he was a successful actor, Hoffman worked in a psychiatric care home. He used his experience there for his role.

2018. Hoffman and Cruise were certain this film would fail.

2019. Ray Bans sunglasses skyrocketed after Tom Cruise wore them in this film.

2020. Most of Hoffman's performance was inspired by Kim Peek, a mentally disabled man with an incredible ability to make huge calculations and remember things in astonishing detail. His nickname was "Kimputer."

Ran
(1985)

2021.　There is one close-up in the film.

2022.　"Ran" is Japanese for "revolution."

2023.　Hundreds of costumes were made by hand. It took two years to make them all.

2024.　The film had 1,400 extras. This means that 1,400 suits of armour had to be created. They were designed by the director, Akira Kurosawa, himself.

2025.　Kurosawa wrote the script ten years before it was released.

2026.　Kurosawa was seventy-six when he directed this.

2027.　This is considered to be Kurosawa's final masterpiece.

2028.　Kurosawa's was nearly blind while making this film. His assistants took care of most of the principal photography.

2029.　The film required 200 horses.

2030.　Akira Kurosawa's wife died during production. He took one day off to mourn.

Rashomon
(1950)

2031. Rashomon popularised a famous story-telling technique called "The Unreliable Narrator." The audience assume that the narrator of a story is always telling the truth but they could be lying.

2032. Most of the cast kept complaining to the director that they didn't understood the story. He told them that they weren't meant to.

2033. Western audiences assumed that Kurosawa copied the structure of Citizen Kane for this film. However, Kurosawa didn't see Citizen Kane until years later.

2034. Kurosawa said that the biggest problem with making the film was the slugs that kept falling from the trees onto the cast and crew.

2035. Toshiro Mifune studied lions for his character.

2036. George Lucas loved Mifune so much in this film that he was considered for Obi-Wan for Star Wars.

2037. The word "Rashomon" was added to the Oxford English Dictionary after this film was released. The word means "being characterized by multiple confliction or differing interpretations."

2038. This film is based off the book, "In a Grove."

2039. Kurosawa poured ink into the rain machine so the "rain" was more visible.

2040. This was the film that made the Academy Awards create the Best Foreign Film category.

Rear Window
(1954)

2041.   Alfred Hitchcock was at his thinnest when he was making this film. He weighed 215lbs. At his maximum, he weighed 365lbs.

2042.   Hitchcock cameos as the man who is winding the clock, thirty minutes into the film.

2043.   Nearly every shot takes place in Jeff's apartment.

2044.   A 1998 remake was made with Christopher Reeve in the title role.

2045.   All of the apartments in Thorwald's building were liveable. They even had electricity and running water.

2046.   One of the actresses lived in her "apartment" for most of the shoot.

2047.   This is the only film that Grace Kelly has starred in where she is holding a cigarette.

2048.   One day, the camera lights got so hot that they set off the sprinklers.

2049.   Since the film was in a set, a thousand lights were used to simulate sunlight.

2050.   Hitchcock only hired Raymond Burr as the villain because he looked like David O. Selznick, a producer Hitchcock hated.

Rebecca
(1940)

2051.   This was the first film Alfred Hitchcock made in Hollywood.

2052.   This was the only film that won Hitchcock a Best Picture Oscar.

2053.   Mrs. de Winter's first name is never revealed.

2054.   Hitchcock told Joan Fontaine that everyone on the set hated her. This made her feel very uncomfortable, which is exactly what Hitchcock wanted for her character.

2055.   Vivien Leigh nearly played the lead.

2056.   Filming started five days after the UK entered WWII. This was awkward as most of the actors were British.

2057.   The producer hated the film so much that he strongly considered terminating the production and cutting his losses.

2058.   Hitchcock cameos at the end. He walks passed the phonebook that Jack Favell is in.

2059.   The producer wanted the film to be identical to the book but Hitchcock made several changes. This is the main reason the two of them clashed.

2060.   In the book, Maxim kills Rebecca on purpose. In the film, he kills her by accident.

Rebel Without a Cause
(1955)

2061. Marlon Brando auditioned for the lead role of an earlier version of the film (1947.) His audition can be viewed on YouTube.

2062. Although James Dean is playing a teenager, he was twenty-four at the time of filming.

2063. T-shirt sales skyrocketed after this film's release.

2064. The entire story takes place within 24 hours.

2065. Paul Newman was considered for the lead.

2066. The film was supposed to contain a scene with James Dean kissing Sal Mineo. Sal played John "Plato" Crawford.

2067. The Danish title for the film is "Wild Blood."

2068. Dean's character is called Stark. In East of Eden, Dean's character is called Trask. "Stark" is an anagram of "Trask."

2069. Dennis Hopper was considered for Plato.

2070. James Dean died on September 30th 1955, a month before the film was released.

Requiem for a Dream
(2000)

2071.   This film popularised the Clint Mansell song, Lux Aeterna. It has been used in many films since. Probably the most famous example is the epic remix that was used for The Lord of the Rings: The Two Towers trailer.

2072.   Giovanni Ribishi was considered for the lead.

2073.   Jared Leto lost 25lbs for the film.

2074.   Ellen Burstyn hated the script and found it pornographic. After she saw the director's previous film, Pi, she realised that the film had a lot of potential.

2075.   The film has many extremely short shots. This was done to make the characters look like their senses were overloaded from all of the drugs they used. An average film has 650 cuts. This film had 2,000.

2076.   Jared Leto became friends with many junkies for preparation for the role.

2077.   Ellen Burstyn said her character in this film was the character she was proudest of.

2078.   The word "heroin" is never said in the film.

2079.   Dave Chappelle turned down the part of Tyrone. The role went to Marlon Wayans.

2080.   When Sara talks about how it feels to be old, the camera drifts off. The reason why this happened is because the cameraman found her speech so moving that he couldn't stop crying. This shot was left in the final cut.

Reservoir Dogs
(1992)

2081.   In the breakfast scene, Quentin Tarantino raises his hand. This was his way of saying "stop the scene" because one of the actors messed up his lines. However, no one else noticed so the scene carried on. This was the shot used for the final film.

2082.   Tim Roth did his audition while he and the director, Quentin Tarantino, were drunk.

2083.   The film's budget was so low that most of the actors had to wear their own clothes.

2084.   The iconic suits that the main actors wear were provided for free by the designer.

2085.   Steve Buscemi and Tim Roth didn't own suit trousers so they wore black jeans with their jackets.

2086.   Tim Roth spent so much time lying in fake blood that it would dry up and he would have to be peeled off.

2087.   Tarantino was going to play Mr. Pink before Buscemi delivered a perfect audition.

2088.   Although Reservoir Dogs is considered to be one of the best heist films ever, Tarantino has pointed out that you never see a heist at any point.

2089.   The European distributors used one-sheet posters for each of the main characters. This was an odd decision at the time but it is extremely common nowadays, especially for blockbusters like the Marvel films.

2090.　Although the ear-removal scene is the most iconic part of the film, Michael Madsen felt extremely uncomfortable doing the scene as he detests violence.

2091.　Tarantino asked James Woods' agent if Woods would be interested in the film. The agent turned down Tarantino five times and didn't mention it to Woods. When Woods eventually found out, he fired his agent.

2092.　Kirk Baltz plays the cop that Mr. Blonde tortures. Baltz wanted to know what it felt like to be kidnapped so he asked Michael Madsen to stuff him in the trunk of his car and drive around.

2093.　Tarantino was going to make the film for $30,000 until he received a phone call from Harvery Keitel, who offered $1.5 million if he could star in it and produce it. Tarantino agreed.

2094.　George Clooney nearly played Mr. Blonde.

2095.　Christopher Walken turned down Mr. Blonde.

2096.　Samuel L. Jackson auditioned for Mr. Orange.

2097.　The film did very badly in America. However, it did so well in England, that Tarantino would be swamped by fans while he was walking the streets.

2098.　Tony Scott really wanted to direct this film.

2099.　Tarantino said that Terry Gilliam gave him a lot of advice for the film.

2100.　Tarantino considered himself to be the most inexperienced person on set.

2101.   When Mr. Pink talks about tipping, he mentions that he worked at a place with minimum wage. He plays a waiter in Tarantino's film, Pulp Fiction.

2102.   The film was completed three days before its release.

2103.   David Duchovny auditioned for a role.

2104.   Mr. Blonde is never seen killing anyone.

2105.   The singer, Pink, said her stage name was inspired from the character, Mr. Pink.

2106.   No dialogue is spoken by a woman.

2107.   When Madsen's character, Mr. Blonde is torturing the cop, he screams that he has a child. Madsen has just become a father and was shaken when this line was said to him. When he pauses, Quentin Tarantino thought he was about to ruin an otherwise perfect take. You can hear Tarantino say, "No, no!" at this point in the scene.

2108.   Nice Guy Eddie is played by Chris Penn. Penn's blood squibs went off early in the final standoff so he had no choice but to fall down early. This was left in the final film.

2109.   SPOILER – There are a few subtle clues on who the "rat" is. At the beginning, when Joe asks who didn't tip, Mr. Orange snitches on Mr. Pink.

2110.   SPOILER – When an orange balloon appears after Nice Guy Eddie talks about the botched crime, eagle-eyed viewers assumed this was a clue that Mr. Orange is the rat. However, Tarantino said it was a complete coincidence.

Rio Bravo
(1959)

2111.   The sets were built $7/8^{th}$ scale so the performers look larger than life.

2112.   Elvis Presley was considered for a role.

2113.   Quentin Tarantino has said that he will never date a girl that doesn't like Rio Bravo.

2114.   Walter Brennan plays the limping character, Stumpy. Throughout filming, he kept forgetting which leg he was supposed to limp on.

2115.   There is no dialogue for the first four minutes.

2116.   Montgomery Clift was offered a part. He refused because he didn't want to work with the vocally homophobic John Wayne.

2117.   There's only two close-ups in the entire film.

2118.   This is John Carpenter's favourite film.

2119.   This was the twenty-second film John Wayne did with Ward Bond. It was also the last film they worked together.

2120.   This was the last film where John Wayne wore the hat he had worn since the 1939 film, Stagecoach.

Rocky
(1976)

2121.   Sylvester Stallone was offered $350,000 by the producers so they could have the rights for the film. However, they stipulated that Stallone was not allowed to star in it. When they made this decision, Stallone had $106, didn't own a car and was strongly considering selling his dog because he couldn't afford dog food. Nevertheless, Stallone refused.

2122.   Although it sounds like the producers were ruthless because they didn't want Stallone to be in the film, they actually had a lot of faith in the script. When the film went over budget, they raised $100,000 themselves by re-mortgaging their houses.

2123.   Sylvester Stallone wrote the first draft in three days.

2124.   The producers desperately wanted Burt Reynolds for the lead part.

2125.   Rocky's name comes from heavyweight boxer, Rocky Marciano. He won forty-nine fights and he was undefeated. His knockout percentage was 88%.

2126.   Cher auditioned for Adrian.

2127.   Rocky was inspired by Chuck Wepner. Wepner fought Muhammad Ali on March 24th 1975. Wepner was considered an ordinary boxer and no one believed he would last longer than three rounds. However, he managed to knock Ali down in the ninth round. Ali eventually won with nineteen seconds left in the fifteenth round but only after he broke Wepner's nose and left huge gashes above his eyes.

2128.   The budget was so tight that the producers wanted to cut the scene where Rocky is in bed crying that he's not good enough. Stallone refused, saying it was the most important scene in the film.

2129.   Rocky's dog is Stallone's actual dog.

2130.   The poster of Rocky VS Apollo shows Rocky wearing red shorts with a white stripe. However, Rocky's shorts are white with a red stripe. Realising they made a mistake, Stallone decided to reference this in his dialogue to show that people care about him so little that they can't even get his outfit right.

2131.   This was the most successful film of 1976.

2132.   It won the Oscar for Best Picture in 1977.

2133.   The photos of Rocky as a boy are actually of a young Stallone.

2134.   Stallone got so out of breath during his training scenes that he had to quit smoking.

2135.   In the meat-locker scene, Stallone punched the slabs so many times that his knuckles are permanently flat.

2136.   The director was John Avildsen. He has never watched a boxing match.

2137.   The director has never seen a boxing film.

2138.   Stallone trained for six months for the role.

2139.   Carl Weathers and Burgess Meredith had to share a small dressing room because the budget was so small.

2140.   The entire film was shot in twenty-eight days.

2141.   Stallone and Carl Weathers couldn't make boxing look interesting on camera. As a result, Stallone had to write out thirty-two pages of choreographed moves in their fight e.g. Rocky throws a left, Creed ducks, Rocky jabs with a right, Creed moves back, etc.

2142.   It took thirty-five hours to shoot the boxing scenes.

2143.   Rocky's real name is Robert.

2144.   Stallone wanted Harvey Keitel to play Paulie.

2145.   Stallone's brother, Frank, cameos as the street band's lead singer.

2146.   Stallone's father, Frankie, cameos as the bell ringer.

2147.   In one scene, Burt Young had to act drunk. An actual drunk wandered on set and told him his performance was unconvincing. Young then copied the drunk's demeanour.

2148.   While shooting the final fight, Stallone suffered bruised ribs and Carl Weathers damaged his nose. Weirdly, their characters had the opposite injuries.

2149.   This was the first sports film to win an Oscar for Best Picture.

2150.   The most expensive part of the film was the make-up.

Roman Holiday
(1953)

2151.   The budget was so tight that the producers had to hire an unknown actress for the Princess. They cast an up-and-coming Belgian actress called Audrey Hepburn. She became one of the biggest stars in Hollywood.

2152.   Peck agreed to star in the film because he had not done a comedy yet.

2153.   Gregory Peck was so certain that Audrey Hepburn was going to win an Oscar, that he told the producers to put her name above the title. They agreed and she won.

2154.   Cary Grant was supposed to play the lead role.

2155.   This was the first American film shot entirely in Italy.

2156.   Hepburn won a Tony for her Broadway performance in Ondine shortly after this film. This makes her one of the only people in history to win an Oscar and a Tony in the same year.

2157.   Elizabeth Taylor was considered for the Princess.

2158.   The interview paper that Hennessy reads is actually the film script.

2159.   It is never revealed what country the Princess is from.

2160.   When Hepburn auditioned, the cameraman shouted "Cut!" but he was instructed to keep filming secretly. When they saw the real Audrey Hepburn, it convinced them she was the right person for the part.

Rope
(1948)

2161.   Hitchcock made this film because he wanted to see if he could do an entire film in one take. At the time, it was impossible because camera reels could only contain ten minutes of footage. As a result, the film is made of ten ten-minute scenes. Hitchcock did his best to disguise the transition from one reel to another so the whole film looks like it was done in one shot.

2162.   The film is eighty minutes long. However, Hitchcock had to mildly speed up some of the scenes to make sure all of the vital dialogue was divulged before the reel ended. If the film was played at normal speed, it would have been one hundred minutes long..

2163.   Because of the long takes, the crew had to be extra dutiful to avoid mistakes. At one point, a camera dolly ran over a cameraman's foot and broke it. He was gagged and dragged off. This was left in the final film.

2164.   One of actresses tried to put her glass down but she missed the table. A crewmember dashed in and caught it before it hit the ground. This was left in the final cut.

2165.   This was Hitchcock's first film in colour.

2166.   The film was banned in several cities in America because of homosexual implications.

2167.   The murder was based off a real-life murder by Nathan Leopold and Richard Loeb.

2168.   In hindsight, Hitchcock dismissed this film as "a stunt."

2169.   The actors thought the actress who played the maid was an actual maid because she was so good at staying in character.

2170.   James Stewart said this is the only Hitchcock film he doesn't like.

Rush

(2013)

2171.   Chris Hemsworth lost over 30lbs to play James Hunt.

2172.   Paul Greengrass was supposed to direct it.

2173.   Russell Crowe was considered for a role.

2174.   The area where Niki Lauda crashed is now known as the Lauda Link.

2175.   Chris Hemsworth said this film effected his career more than anything else.

2176.   Ron Howard admitted that he knew nothing about Formula One when he became the director of this film.

2177.   Daniel Bruhl had to wear a dental appliance to emulate Niki Lauda's overbite.

2178.   Niki Lauda was astounded by how similar Bruhl looked like him when he saw the film.

2179.   Lauda said the film was completely accurate with portraying his voice, posture, personality and personal events.

2180.   Hemsworth and Bruhl were not allowed to drive Formula One cars for the film.

Scarface
(1983)

2181. This is a remake of the 1932 film of the same name.

2182. Robert De Niro turned down the role of Tony Montana.

2183. When Tony is in the bathtub, he says, "Look at dem pelicangs fly." He had to say this all of the time when he was practising his Cuban accent.

2184. Although some sources say that dried milk was used to portray the cocaine, the director said it's not true. It is unknown what substance was used for the cocaine.

2185. Tony only says one thing in Spanish.

2186. Steven Spielberg shot the last scene.

2187. Miriam Colon played Tony's mother. In reality, she is only four years older than Al Pacino.

2188. Sidney Lumet was supposed to direct the film.

2189. John Travolta was considered for a role.

2190. Tony's "little friend" is an M16 assault rifle with an M203 40mm grenade launcher.

Schindler's List
(1993)

2191.   This is the only film that Steven Spielberg has ever won a Best Director Oscar.

2192.   Claire Danes was considered for an unspecified role.

2193.   The film is based off the Thomas Keneally novel, Schindler's Ark.

2194.   Spielberg made this film for free. He thought that if he got paid, it would be "blood money."

2195.   Spielberg's salary was donated to the Shoah Foundation.

2196.   Mel Gibson was interested in playing Oscar Schindler.

2197.   Kevin Costner was considered for the lead.

2198.   Ralph Fiennes was cast as the villain, Amon Goeth, because of his "evil sexuality."

2199.   Ralph Fiennes put on 30lbs for the film by drinking lots of Guinness.

2200.   Mila Pfefferberg was a Holocaust survivor. When she met Ralph Fiennes, she started to shake uncontrollably because he looked so much like Amon Goeth.

2201.   When Spielberg showed a cut of the film to composer, John Williams, he said, "You need to get a better composer." Spielberg replied with, "I know. But they're all dead."

2202.   20,000 extras were needed for the film.

2203.   Although Spielberg obtained permission to shoot inside Auschwitz, he refused to out of respect to the victims.

2204.   Harrison Ford turned down the lead role.

2205.   Spielberg said this is the film he is proudest of.

2206.   No green paint or green clothes were used in the film as the colour didn't look right in black-and-white.

2207.   Spielberg watched Seinfeld every night while he was filming to stay positive.

2208.   Spielberg strongly considered making the film in German and Polish.

2209.   Ben Kingsley played the accountant, Itzhak Stern. He kept a picture of Anne Frank in his pocket during his scenes. He eventually played Anne Frank's father, Otto, in Anne Frank: The Whole Story.

2210.   Spielberg refuses to autograph anything connected to this film.

2211.   Spielberg would ring up Robin Williams in-between shots and ask him to do some of his stand-up material. He would then put him on loudspeaker and Robin Williams would entertain the cast and crew.

2212. Bruno Ganz was offered the part of Oskar Schindler. Ironically, he is most famous for playing Adolf Hitler in Downfall.

2213. Dustin Hoffman nearly played the part of Stern.

2214. Liam Neeson doesn't think he's very good in this film.

2215. This is the most expensive black-and-white film ever.

2216. Ralph Fiennes and Liam Neeson's characters pretend to be friends but they scheme behind each others back. Coincidentally, they had the exact same relationship in the film, Clash of the Titans.

2217. Tim Roth was considered for Amon Goeth.

2218. This is the most successful black-and-white film ever, making $96 million. In today's money, that's $321 million.

2219. This is #6 on the top 250 greatest films ever on IMDB.

2220. The girl in the red coat was called Roma Ligocka. She survived the war and wrote a book called The Girl in the Red Coat: A Memoir.

Saving Private Ryan
(1998)

2221.   Many up-and-coming actors were in this film such as Bryan Cranston, Paul Giamatti, Nathan Fillion and Vin Diesel.

2222.   Real amputees had to be used for shots of people missing limbs.

2223.   Spielberg wanted an unknown actor to portray Ryan so he cast Matt Damon. He had no idea Damon would become an Oscar winner for Good Will Hunting shortly before this film was released.

2224.   The camera shakes when something explodes in a scene. This camera shake was done by attaching drills to the camera and turning them on at the same time as the explosion.

2225.   Harrison Ford was considered for the lead role.

2226.   Edward Norton had to turn down the lead role to work on American History X.

2227.   Forty barrels of fake blood were used for the Omaha Beach scene.

2228.   Caparzo was written for Vin Diesel.

2229.   Christopher Eccleston turn down a role for the film.

2230.   Joshua Jackson nearly played Wade.

2231.   Spielberg reduced the colour saturation by 60% to make the film look grimmer.

2232.   When the film aired on television, many tv networks received complaints that there was something wrong with the colour on their television, not realising that the film was supposed to have dark colours.

2233.   The film is banned in Malaysia, due to its violence.

2234.   One of the actors was a German veteran during the Normandy invasion. He had to drop out of the film because he kept freaking out how realistic it was.

2235.   Mel Gibson wanted the lead role.

2236.   The main cast had to go through a horrific week-long boot camp.

2237.   Matt Damon didn't go through boot camp. Spielberg did this so the rest of the cast would resent him, just like their characters would.

2238.   The Omaha Beach scene required 1,000 extras.

2239.   The Omaha Beach scene cost $11 million.

2240.   Spielberg personally operated the camera during the Omaha Beach scene.

2241.   Neil Patrick Harris was considered for Ryan.

2242.   One of the amputees at the start of the film is missing his left arm. However, he can be seen picking up a right arm.

2243.   The Omaha Beach scene was heavily inspirational for the video game, Medal of Honour. Some of the game has the exact same dialogue.

2244.   255 people die in the film.

2245.   The Omaha Beach scene was shot in sequence.

2246.   Every actor in the film is white.

2247.   This is George W. Bush's favourite film.

2248.   Michael Madsen was offered the part of Horvath but he said that Tom Sizemore would be better suited for it.

2249.   Tom Sizemore was battling a drug addiction during production. Spielberg said that he had to have a blood test every day. If he failed one test, he would be fired and replaced with someone else, even if it was at the end of production.

2250.   If Tom Sizemore were fired, he would've been replaced with Billy Bob Thornton.

Se7en
(1995)

2251.   Denzel Washington turned down Brad Pitt's part because the script was "too dark and evil."

2252.   Although they are only seen briefly, all of John Doe's books are real. It took two months to write them all out and it cost $15,000.

2253.   All of the building numbers in the opening scene begin with "7."

2254.   Christina Applegate turned down the role of Tracey.

2255.   Robert Duvall turned down the role of the D.A.

2256.   The delivery at the end of the film was at 7pm.

2257.   Brad Pitt made $7 million.

2258.   At first, Morgan Freeman would draw his hand with his finger on the trigger. Police officers on set approached him to tell him that a cop would never do that.

2259.   The executives hated the ending but Brad Pitt refused to do the film if it was changed.

2260.   In the alternative ending, Mills shoots Doe so that Somerset can continue having a career.

Seven Samurai
(1954)

2261.   This is considered to be the first action film.

2262.   This is considered to be Akira Kurosawa's best film.

2263.   The film has become iconic for creating many concepts on how to tell a story on film. The story revolves around seven over-the-hill samurai who have to band together to stop bandits from attacking a poor village. They argue a lot but, by the end, they have a deep respect for each other. This concept has been done in many other films since like Se7en and The Expendables trilogy.

2264.   Each of the seven is based off actual samurai.

2265.   Kurosawa normally used one camera for his films. However, this was the first film Kurosawa made that required multiple cameras.

2266.   The film is set in 1586.

2267.   Production was shut down multiple times. Kurosawa had to personally argue with the board of directors to convince them that the film was not a flop.

2268.   This is considered to be the greatest Japanese film ever made.

2269.   The studio nearly went bankrupt due to funding this film and Godzilla simultaneously.

2270.   This film gave Kurosawa his reputation as the "World's Greatest Editor."

The Seventh Seal
(1957)

2271. This is the film that Ingmar Bergman was proudest of.

2272. The main character's name, Antonius Block, is only said twice.

2273. Death has been parodied many times, especially by The Grim Reaper in Bill and Ted's Bogus Journey where he plays a board game against the main characters. In this film, he plays Chess. In Bill and Ted, he plays Clue, Battleship and Twister.

2274. This film made Max von Sydow an established actor worldwide.

2275. This is one of thirteen films that von Sydow did with Bergman.

2276. The acting in the film is theatrical-based rather than film-based.

2277. The story was originally written as a play.

2278. The chess pieces were eventually sold at an auction for $145,000.

2279. The church that Block arrives at fifteen minutes into the film is just a model hanging in the dead tree.

2280. The title comes from a Biblical quotation from The Revelation of St. John the Divine, Chapter 8.

The Shawshank Redemption
(1994)

2281.   The Shawshank Redemption is rated as the #1 greatest film of all time on IMDB with a total score of 9.3/10.

2282.   Although IMDB considers it to be the greatest film ever, it has one clear flaw... none of the actors seem to age.

2283.   This film is based off Stephen King's short story, Rita Hayworth and Shawshank Redemption.

2284.   Frank Darabont directed this film. Coincidentally, he adapted another Stephen King novel, The Green Mile.

2285.   In Denmark, the title is "A World Outside."

2286.   This is the film Morgan Freeman is proudest of.

2287.   Red and Dufresne first speak while Red is pitching a ball. This chat took nine hours to shoot. Morgan Freeman pitched the ball so many times that he had to wear a sling the next day.

2288.   Stephen King sold the film rights to his novel for $5,000.

2289.   Charlie Sheen was considered for Andy Dufresne.

2290.   Clint Eastwood was considered for Red.

2291.   Red is supposed to be Irish. Morgan Freeman says this in a film as a joke.

2292.   Rob Reiner was desperate to direct the film. He wanted Harrison Ford to play Red and Tom Cruise to play Dufresne.

2293.   In the beginning, when Dufresne has the revolver in his hands, the hands actually belong to the director.

2294.   Brad Pitt was supposed to play Tommy but he was busy making Interview with the Vampire.

2295.   Andy Dufresne actually appears in another Stephen King novel called Apt Pupil.

2296.   The song that Dufresne plays over the loudspeakers is called Canzonetta sull'aria from Mozart's "Marriage of Figaro."

2297.   In the novel, it details that Red is in jail because he killed his wife, his neighbour's wife and his neighbour's son.

2298.   In Taiwan, the film is called "Fantastic."

2299.   Tim Robbins had to spend time in solitary confinement for the role.

2300.   The Rita Hayworth film the prisoners watch is Gilda.

2301.   The film was nominated for seven Oscars. It didn't win anything.

2302.   In Italy, the film is called "The Wings of Freedom."

2303.   In Israel, the film is called "Walls of Hope."

2304.   In Romania, the film is called "Angel's Hope."

2305.   In Mexico, the film is called "Dreams of Escape."

2306.   The pictures of Red as a young man attached to his parole papers are of Morgan Freeman's son, Alfonso.

2307.   Freeman's son cameos in the film as a con shouting, "Fresh fish! Fresh fish today! We're reeling 'em in!"

2308.   The film made very little money in the cinema.

2309.   Kevin Costner wanted to star in this film but he was busy making Waterworld.

2310.   Tom Hanks wanted to play Dufresne but he was in pre-production for Forrest Gump.

The Shining
(1980)

2311.   Shelley Duvall had to do the scene where she ran up the staircase thirty-five times. That is the equivalent of running up the entire Empire State Building.

2312.   Shelley Duvall was so exhausted from the film, she suffered hair loss.

2313.   The scene where the blood pours out of the elevator took nine days to set up and was done in three takes.

2314.   The snow in the maze was made of 900 tons of salt and crushed Styrofoam.

2315.   The film inspired the documentary, Room 237. This documentary details the potential meanings of The Shining. It was panned by critics and Kubrick's assistant, Leon Vitali, said it was "gibberish."

2316.   Since Kubrick didn't like The Shining film, he was looking forward to the documentary, Room 237. He gave up halfway because it was poorly made.

2317.   The director of Room 237 doesn't believe in any of the nine theories put forward in the film.

2318.   Jack Nicholson hates cheese sandwiches. When Kubrick learned of this, he had them on set every day and made Nicholson eat them, believing that it would make him more agitated in his scenes.

2319.   Jack Nicholson ad-libbed the "little pigs" bit.

2320.   The novel has a sequel called Doctor Sleep.

Shutter Island
(2010)

2321.   The original title for the film was "Ashecliff". This is the name of the asylum.

2322.   Martin Scorsese screened Vertigo for the cast and crew so they would have an idea what style Scorsese was aiming for.

2323.   Josh Brolin was considered for the role of Chuck. The part went to Mark Ruffalo.

2324.   This is the only film that Leonardo DiCaprio and Martin Scorsese made that was not nominated for any Oscars.

2325.   The title is an anagram of "Truths and Lies."

2326.   There are intentional continuity errors throughout the film to foreshadow the ending.

2327.   Rachel Solando is an anagram of Dolores Chanal. This is never mentioned in the film.

2328.   Memento heavily inspired this film.

2329.   It took four months to shoot the film.

2330.   David Fincher was considered for the director.

The Silence of the Lambs
(1991)

2331.   Many reports say that Anthony Hopkins doesn't blink during his scenes. This is untrue.

2332.   Lecter does blink but very rarely. Hopkins said he got this idea from a friend he knew from London who made others feel uncomfortable because he rarely blinked.

2333.   This film is the second time that Hannibal Lecter has been depicted in a film. Brian Cox portrayed Lecter in the film, Manhunter.

2334.   Hopkins studied countless files of serial killers to prepare himself for the role.

2335.   Jack Nicholson was considered for the lead role.

2336.   Halle Berry auditioned for Clarice Starling.

2337.   Jodie Foster tried to buy the rights for the film as soon as she read the novel.

2338.   The film rights were bought by Gene Hackman.

2339.   In the novel, Lecter has six fingers on his left hand.

2340.   The moth on the poster has a skull on its back. This skull was formed from seven women's bodies and is based off Salvador Dali's work.

Sin City
(2005)

2341.   The film is based off the graphic novels, The Hard Goodbye, The Big Fat Kill and That Yellow Bastard. Each of these titles are said at some point during the film.

2342.   The writer, Frank Miller, believed that this story couldn't work as a film. Robert Rodriguez invited him to look at a rehearsal. When Miller arrived, he realised that it wasn't a rehearsal; it was the first day of shooting! Luckily, Miller was won over by Rodriguez passion and allowed him to direct the film.

2343.   Even though Brittany Murphy appears in all three stories, she shot all of her scenes in one day.

2344.   The writer, Frank Miller, cameos as the priest Marv kills.

2345.   Four actors were replaced for the sequel, Sin City: A Dame to Kill For.
        Josh Brolin replaced Clive Owen as Dwight because Owen was committed to a television series.
        Dennis Haybert replaced Michael Clarke Duncan as Manute after Duncan passed away.
        Jeremy Piven replaced Michael Madsen as Bob because the director believed that Piven would be better suited for this story.
        Jamie Chung replace Devon Aoki as Miho because Aoki was pregnant.
        Brittany Murphy's character, Shellie, was written out because Murphy died.

2346.   Many actors who share scenes never met each other. Mickey Rourke and Elijah Wood didn't meet until after the film was released even thought they have two fight scenes.

2347. Many people commended the makeup of Benicio Del Toro's makeup, saying that it was so subtle that they forgot that he doesn't looks like that.

2348. Johnny Depp was supposed to play Jackie Boy.

2349. Leonardo DiCaprio was supposed to play Junior.

2350. The katana that Miho used was the same blade used by The Bride in Kill Bill.

2351. Elijah Wood's chin was altered in post-production to make him have a more unsettling look.

2352. In the graphic novel, Cardinal Roark is a dwarf and Marv is 7ft tall. In reality, Mickey Rourke, who played Marv, is two inches shorter than Rutger Hauer, who played Roark.

2353. Nick Stahl played Yellow Bastard. Because he was filmed in front of a greenscreen, he had to be painted blue, as the colour yellow didn't look right in a greenscreen. On set, he was known as Blue Bastard.

2354. Christopher Walken was considered for Senator Roark.

2355. Michael Madsen was considered for Marv.

2356. Jessica Simpson auditioned for Nancy.

2357. Adrien Brody auditioned for Jackie Boy.

2358. Uma Thurman was considered for Lucille.

2359.   Kate Bosworth was considered for Gail.

2360.   Nick Offerman has a small part in the film as Shlubb. He is more well known nowadays for playing Ron Swanson in Parks and Recreation.

Singin' in the Rain
(1952)

2361.   Gene Kelly had a fever of 101 when he performed the Singin' in the Rain sequence.

2362.   All of the songs were written first and then the plot had to be written around them.

2363.   Gene Kelly was a nightmare to work with. He was so good at dancing, that he couldn't tolerate anything except perfection.

2364.   This was the sixth film to use the song "Singin' in the Rain."

2365.   After the Make 'em Laugh dance, Donald O' Connor was so tired that he went to bed for three days.

2366.   Debbie Reynolds had to rub her eyes with onions for her crying scene.

2367.   Gene Kelly told Debbie Reynolds that she couldn't dance. She ran away and hid under a piano and cried. Luckily, Fred Astaire saw her and agreed to help her with her dancing.

2368.   Debbie Reynolds lived so far away that she sometimes slept on set.

2369.   The original negative was destroyed in a fire.

2370.   When Gene Kelly does the "Singin' in the Rain" scene, it wasn't decided where he was going to move and he was so ill, the director wanted to send him home. Nevertheless, he ad-libbed most of the song and did it in one take. This take was used for the final cut.

The Sixth Sense
(1999)

2371.   M. Night Shyamalan said he cast Haley Joel Osment because –
i)   He did the best audition
ii)   He wore a tie
iii)   He read the script three times the night before.

2372.   Donnie Wahlberg lost 43lbs for his role as Vincent Grey, the deranged man in the film's opening scene.

2373.   Toni Collette found the script so touching that she didn't think it was a horror film until she saw it.

2374.   The film was shot in sequence.

2375.   Shyamalan cameos as a doctor.

2376.   This is the most rented VHS and DVD ever.

2377.   The voice on Vincent's session that makes Dr. Crowe realise that the ghosts are real is speaking Spanish. It translates into, "Please, I don't want to die Lord, save me, save me."

2378.   This was the first film Michael Cera ever auditioned for. He auditioned for the lead.

2379.   Bruce Willis' character was originally a crime scene photographer.

2380.   The Chinese title for this film gives away the twist!

Slumdog Millionaire
(2008)

2381.   The excrement in the toilet scene was made of peanut butter and chocolate.

2382.   The screenwriter had to visit India three times to get a feel of India.

2383.   The three child actors will not get paid until they are sixteen. The director, Danny Boyle, put their fee in a trust fund until they are old enough to spend the money maturely.

2384.   Danny Boyle wanted Kayn Banega Crorepati to play the game show host. Kayn is the game show host of the Indian version of Who Wants to Be a Millionaire?

2385.   Anil Kapoor plays the game show host. He was a contestant on the show and won 5 million Rupees.

2386.   Some viewers considered "Slumdog" as a racist term. However, Danny Boyle said it was referencing the phrase "underdog."

2387.   The film is based off the book, 50/50.

2388.   The film was nearly released straight to DVD.

2389.   20% of the film was in Hindi.

2390.   The jackpot of the game show is 20 million Rupees. This is the equivalent of $411,600 (or £270,709.)

Snatch
(2000)

2391. Brad Pitt loved Guy Ritchie's film, Lock, Stock and Two Smoking Barrels and told the director that he would love to be in his next film. However, Pitt couldn't do a London accent. When Ritchie asked him what accent he could do, Pitt showed him his Irish accent. This indirectly created the Irish gypsy story line.

2392. Some critics complained that they couldn't understand the accents or slang in Ritchie's previous film. Ritchie countered this by making, Mickey's accent almost indecipherable.

2393. Most deaths in the film are off-screen.

2394. Stand-ins had to be used for some of Bullet-Tooth's scenes because Vinnie Jones was usually in jail throughout the shoot.

2395. The producers couldn't afford enough extras for the boxing scenes so the extras had to keep moving around when the camera angle shifted.

2396. Frankie Four Fingers changes his outfit four times while he is talking to Avi.

2397. Sean Connery was supposed to play Brick Top.

2398. Guy Ritchie appears as a man reading the newspaper in the first scene with Doug the Head.

2399. Twenty-six people die in the film.

2400. In the final scene, the 86-carat diamond is called an 84-carat diamond.

Some Like It Hot
(1959)

2401.   This is often considered to be the funniest film ever made.

2402.   It took forty-three takes for Marilyn Monroe to say, "It's me, Sugar" correctly.

2403.   Monroe was known for requiring at least thirty takes to do the simplest task. In one scene, Monroe has to rummage through drawers and said, "Where's the bourbon?" She did it forty times and would say things like, "Where's the bonbon?" In the end, the director had to write the line inside the drawer she opens.

2404.   Tony Curtis and Jack Lemmon wore their female costumes around the studio and even in the ladies room to see if they could pass as women. No one said a thing.

2405.   During the first preview, many people walked out halfway through the film, saying it was dreadful. When the director, was asked what needs to be cut or changed, he said, "Nothing."

2406.   The film had to be in black-and-white as Lemmon and Curtis' female makeup wouldn't look right on a colour camera.

2407.   Throughout the shoot, Monroe was often two or three hours late and would sometimes not leave her dressing room.

2408.   Monroe was pregnant throughout the shoot, which was why she was so nervous. Because she was noticeably heavier for the film, a lot of the posters had her head superimposed on another model's body.

2409.   This film was banned in Kansas for being "too disturbing." Don't ask why.

2410.   The film was nearly called "Not Tonight Josephine."

The Sound of Music
(1965)

2411.   Julie Andrews learned to play the guitar for this film.

2412.   Christopher Plummer's singing was dubbed.

2413.   Grace Kelly was considered for the Baroness.

2414.   This is Seth MacFarlane's favourite film. He has spoofed it many times in his television show, Family Guy.

2415.   Plummer was drunk throughout most of filming.

2416.   If this film didn't do well, 20th Century Fox would've gone bankrupt after they lost so much money on the 1963 film, Cleopatra.

2417.   This film was in the VHS charts for five years consistently.

2418.   A very young Kurt Russell auditioned for one of the Von Trapp children.

2419.   Richard Dreyfus auditioned for one of the Von Trapp children but he didn't get the role because he couldn't dance.

2420.   Christopher Plummer hates this film.

Spartacus
(1960)

2421. Dalton Trumbo wrote this script. However, he wasn't supposed to be credited because he was on the Hollywood blacklist for being a Communist. As a result, the director, Stanley Kubrick, said he would pretend that he wrote it. The lead actor, Kirk Douglas, refused to accept this and demanded that Trumbo be credited. As a result, the Hollywood blacklist was disbanded.

2422. Peter Ustinov won a Best Supporting Actor Oscar for the film. He is the only person to have won an Oscar for a Kubrick film.

2423. Ingrid Bergman auditioned for Varinia.

2424. To make big actors agree to star in the film, Douglas showed them different versions of the script where their character was heavily emphasised.

2425. Orson Welles was considered for a role.

2426. Despite what the film depicts, Spartacus was a free man in real life.

2427. Laurence Olivier wears a false nose for his character, Crassus.

2428. Kubrick thought the famous, "I Am Spartacus" scene was stupid.

2429. 10,500 people were in the film.

2430. Kubrick hated that he wasn't in complete control of the film. As a result, he had total control of every film he directed for the remainder of his career.

Spirited Away
(2001)

2431.   This is considered the greatest animated film made in Japan or Studio Ghibli or by Hayao Miyazaki.

2432.   This was the first anime to win an Oscar.

2433.   This is the highest rated animated film on IMDB.

2434.   This was the first film directed by Miyazaki where a child character is voiced by a child.

2435.   There are references to pigs, gorging and dust bunnies in this film. These are reoccurring traits in Miyazaki's work.

2436.   No Face is based off a silkworm.

2437.   There is references to the Biblical story, Sodom and Gomorrah (in terms of "not looking back.")

2438.   There is references to the Greek myth, Orpheus and Eurydice.

2439.   The executive producer of PIXAR, John Lasseter, supervised this film.

2440.   The jumping lamp at Zeniba's house is a reference to the PIXAR logo.

Stagecoach
(1939)

2441. Orson Welles watched this film forty times while he was making Citizen Kane.

2442. Most of the sets had ceilings, which was very rare for films of the time. This inspired Orson Welles to do the same thing for Citizen Kane.

2443. John Wayne's hat is his own.

2444. Local Navajo Indians played the Apaches.

2445. This was the director's first sound Western.

2446. This was the first sound Western in thirteen years.

2447. The director was John Ford. This was the first of many collaborations with him and John Wayne.

2448. A local shaman called Hosteen Tso promised the director that the cloud formations he needed for the film would appear. He was right.

2449. The director was asked, "Why didn't the Indians just shoot the horses in the film's climax?" His reply was, "Because that would have been the end of the movie."

2450. This was John Wayne's eightieth film.

Stand by Me
(1986)

2451.   Stephen King says this film is his favourite adaption of any of his books.

2452.   The cigarettes the children smoke are made from cabbage leaves.

2453.   Corey Feldman said his character, Teddy, was the character that had the most similarities to his own personality.

2454.   The leech scene actually happened to Stephen King as a child.

2455.   The character, Teddy, appeared in Carrie, another King novel.

2456.   Ace appears in King's novel, Needless Things.

2457.   The film was nearly called "The Body."

2458.   The Shawshank Prison is referenced by the characters. This is an obvious reference to King's novel, Rita Hayworth and the Shawshank Redemption.

2459.   The vomit was made from cottage cheese and blueberry mix.

2460.   One day, the cast and crew went to a fair and bought some cookies. They didn't realise that they were pot cookies and a lot of the cast and crew became heavily stoned.

Star Trek
(2009)

2461. Abrams asked George Lucas how he could make the film better. Lucas's answer was, "Lightsabers."

2462. This was Chris Hemsworth's film debut.

2463. Zachary Quinto couldn't do the Vulcan salute for his role as Spock. He had to have his hands superglued for the scene.

2464. Zachary Quinto and Leonard Nimoy both play Spock. Since Quinto was taller than Nimoy, they had to use specific camera angles to hide the difference.

2465. The automatic doors opening on the Enterprise was made from a train toilet flushing.

2466. The sound effect made from Kirk's motorcycle is the same sound effect used in The Jetsons for the flying cars.

2467. Steven Spielberg convinced J.J. Abrams to take the job as director.

2468. Russell Crowe nearly played the villain, Nero.

2469. When Sulu stabs a Romulan, green blood spills out. This is because Vulcans' blood is based off copper, not iron.

2470. Simon Pegg didn't audition. He was offered the part. Pegg said he would've paid Abrams to be in the film.

Star Wars
(1977)

2471. The first draft has almost no resemblance to the finished product. The story was originally supposed to revolve around the Jedi, Mace Windu. Mace was eventually played by Samuel L. Jackson in Star Wars: Episode 1 – The Phantom Menace. Hans Solo was a green gilled noseless alien. Luke Skywalker was a sixty-year old general called Starkiller. Lucas also wanted a dwarf to be one of the main characters.

2472. The Millenium Falcon's design is based off a hamburger with a bite taken out of it.

2473. George Lucas didn't attend the premier because he was so certain the film would fail.

2474. The film concludes with Luke venturing into the Meridian Trench of the Death Star. However, the Trench only existed because the model maker, Colin Cantwell, was lazy. The material used to craft the Death Star tended to shrink and the final model had a gap in the middle. When Cantwell was asked to fix it, he said they could just explain why it was like that in the plot. This act of laziness became the final battle scene.

2475. The actors who played C-3PO (Anthony Daniels) and R2-D2 (Kenny Baker) didn't get on at all. They did admit after filming that they didn't have a genuine problem with each other and they were simply frustrated by being stuck in uncomfortable costumes all of the time.

2476. The distant shots of Luke's landspeeder aren't of the actors, but of dolls wrapped in robes.

2477.   The gigantic alien skeleton in Tattooine was left in the desert by the crew. When they had to return to the area in the year, 2000 to make Star Wars: Episode II – Attack of the Clones, it was still there twenty-three years later.

2478.   The film was nearly cancelled on the very first day when Tunisia experienced its worst desert storm in half a century, destroying most of the set.

2479.   Peter Cushing played Grand Moff Tarkin (the man who gives the order to destroy Alderaan.) He found his boots so uncomfortable, that he begged Lucas to shoot his scenes from the waist up as often as possible. In every scene where Moff can only be seen from the waist up, Cushing is wearing slippers. Fuzzy ones.

2480.   Christopher Walken was the main contender to play Hans Solo.

2481.   R2-D2 had English dialogue written for him so all of C-3PO's reactions to him would seem more genuine.

2482.   Before the film's release, Lucas showed a rough cut to Steven Spielberg, Francis Ford Coppola and Brian De Palma. Coppola thought it was a disaster. De Palma said it was the "worst picture ever." Spielberg was the only one who had faith in it and said "it will make a fortune."

2483.   The lightsaber sound was crated from the hum of an idling 35mmm movie projector and the feedback generated by passing a stripped microphone cable by a television.

2484.   The Banthas were Asian elephants wearing fur costumes and fake horns.

2485. Princess Leia and Obi-Wan Kenobi never meet during the film.

2486. Peter Mayhew played the Wookiee, Chewbacca. He won the part ten seconds into the audition. He said that got the part as soon as he stood up. He is 7ft 2.

2487. Studio executives were uncomfortable with the fact that Chewbacca is naked.

2488. Dave Prowse played Darth Vader. James Earl Jones provided the voice of Vader. Jones wasn't credited for Vader because he didn't want to be typecast as a sci-fi villain.

2489. Dave Prowse's Welsh accent was so thick that the film crew called him Darth Farmer.

2490. Prowse had no idea that his voice was going to be dubbed until the film's release.

2491. James Earl Jones and Dave Prowse have never met.

2492. Mark Hamill, who played Luke Skywalker, was trying to make sure his hair matched up in every shot for the sake of continuity. When Harrison Ford learned this, he said, "Kid, it's not that kind of movie."

2493. Many sources say that Alec Guinness, who played Obi-Wan, hated the film. However, he found the film "staggering as spectacle and technically brilliant, exciting, very noisy and warm-hearted. The battle scenes at the end go on for minutes too long, and some of the dialogue is excruciating and much of it is lost in noise, but it remains a vivid experience."

2494. All of the Stormtroopers are left-handed.

2495.   To make it look like he was about to be crushed for the trash compactor scene, Mark Hamill held his breath. However, he held his breath for so long, that he broke a blood vessel in his face. Subsequent shots are from one side only.

2496.   The Empire has 25,000 Star Destroyers.
Each Star Destroyer contains –
9,235 officers
27,850 enlisted
9,700 Stormtroopers
That means that the Empire has 1.1 billion people serving them.

2497.   A research study in Washington University worked out that the Death Star would've cost approximately $200 quintillion to construct. That's $200,000,000,000,000,000,000,000.

2498.   The sound of the Star Destroyer's engine was a broken air conditioner.

2499.   The Jawas language is Zulu on fast-forward.

2500.   Greedo's voice is the Quechuan language (Peruvian Indian) backwards.

Star Wars: Episode V - The Empire Strikes Back
(1980)

2501.   Although it is considered to be the best film of the trilogy, it wasn't too popular in its time. Although critics praised Star Wars, many complained that Empire was too dark and it wasn't as fun as the last one.

2502.   Before filming, Mark Hamill was involved in a car accident and his face was scarred. Some sources say that the scene where he is hit in the face by a Wampa was added in to explain why Luke had facial scars. This isn't true. At the time of shooting, Hamill had no visible scars on his face.

2503.   The sound of Vader's shuttle door opening is a recording of a whole block of prison cell doors slamming shut.

2504.   Lucas loved Frank Oz' depiction of Yoda so much that he spent thousands of dollars trying to get him nominated for an Oscar. Sadly, the academy didn't consider a puppeteer to be an actor. Although Lucas was furious, Oz didn't mind.

2505.   Frank Oz famously worked on The Muppets series. He would do Yoda in the voice as Miss Piggy when Mark Hamill would get frustrated.

2506.   There is a shoe in the Asteroid scene.

2507.   There is a potato in the Asteroid scene.

2508.   Yoda's speech pattern is in Object-Subject-Verb order. This is based off Amazonian languages.

2509.   Boba Fett has four lines.

2510. Boba Fett is never referred to by name.

2511. The AT-AT's were inspired by the machines in H.G. Wells's novel, War of the Worlds.

2512. Vader's Super Star Destroyer is called Executor.

2513. The creature that the Millennium Falcon hides in is called Exgorth. Inside Exgorth is an alien called a Mynock. The sounds that the Mynock makes was a recording of a horse neighing being played backwards.

2514. Yoda was supposed to be called Minch.

2515. Yoda's face was based off Albert Einstein.

2516. Billy Dee Williams played Lando. He auditioned to play Hans Solo.

2517. The sounds the Tauntauns make were recordings of Asian sea otters.

2518. Lucas considers this to be the worst film in the series. He even apologised for it when it was released. It is ranked #12 on IMDB's top 250 greatest films ever made. It is the highest ranking Star Wars film and is often considered one of the best, if not, the greatest film ever made.

2519. This is the first film to star Vader's master, The Emperor. He is played by a hooded old woman with superimposed chimpanzee eyes and was voiced by Clive Reville. Ian McDiarmid played him the sequel.

2520. In the Italian version, Vader's name was "Fener." This is because "Vader" means "toilet" in Italian.

2521.   The blizzard on the planet, Hoth, wasn't a special effect.

2522.   Lando was supposed to be a clone that survived that Clone Wars.

2523.   When Vader's helmet lowers onto his body, the sound effect is from a person putting their hand over a vacuum tube.

2524.   Yoda was going to be played by a monkey wearing an alien-like mask. Pictures of it can be found online.

2525.   Carrie Fisher had to stand on a box in her scenes with Ford because she was a foot shorter than him.

2526.   Hans Solo was frozen in carbonite because Harrison Ford wasn't sure if he wanted to do a sequel.

2527.   Lando wears Hans Solo's clothes in the last scene.

2528.   The stormtroopers's uniforms weren't built from long-lasting material, which made the white paint flake. Lucas worried that this would make them look amateur. On the contrary, fans liked the flaked look because it made their uniforms look battle-worn.

2529.   Harrison Ford ad-libbed the famous line, "I know" when Leia says, "I love you."

2530.   No one knew the film's twist apart from James Earl Jones and Mark Hamill and a few crew members. Hamill was only told the twist minutes before he shot the scene. Not even the actor who played Darth Vader knew the twist because he was given a false line. He said, "Obi-Wan killed your father."

Star Wars: Episode VI – Return of the Jedi
(1983)

2531.   The dancer that Jabba drops into the Rancor pit lost her top as she fell in.

2532.   Dave Prowse played Darth Vader for the first half of the film. For the second half, he was played by his stunt double, Bob Anderson.

2533.   This was the first film that James Earl Jones was credited for the voice of Vader.

2534.   Seven actors played Darth Vader throughout the six films.
Jake Lloyd played him as a child in Episode I.
Hayden Christensen played Vader in Episode II and III.
Dave Prowse played him in Episode IV-VI.
James Earl Jones provided the voice in Episode III-VI.
Bob Anderson performed the swordfights as Vader in Episode V-VI.
Sebastian Shaw was the face of Vader in Episode VI.
Vader's breathing was done by George Lucas himself.

2535.   Sebastian Shaw had no idea that he would be playing Darth Vader until the day he shot the scene.

2536.   It took six puppeteers to control Jabba the Hutt.

2537.   Jabba was supposed to be a hairy creature but Lucas changed his mind as Jabba would've been too similar to Chewbacca.

2538. Alec Guinness shot his scene in one day.

2539. In the scene where Salacious Crumb is eating C-3PO's eye, the actor, Anthony Daniels had a panic attack due to the claustrophobia he felt being in the costume. This was the shot used for the film.

2540. Lando's co-pilot, Nien Nunb speaks in a Kenyan dialect known as Haya.

2541. Alan Rickman auditioned for the controller of the Death Starr, Moff Jerjerrod.

2542. Admiral Ackbar's famous line, "It's a trap!" was supposed to be "It's a trick!"

2543. Admiral Ackbar used to be a slave of Moff Tarkin (the Death Star's leader in the first film.) He was forced to be his personal pilot. This backstory never got into the final film.

2544. The sounds the Rancor makes are from a dachshund.

2545. Lucas wanted The Emperor to sound posh. However, the actor, Ian McDiarmid showed Lucas the voice he wanted to do and Lucas loved it. McDiarmid based the Emperor's voice on a Japanese method of using your stomach to project your voice into a guttural croak.

2546. Although The Emperor's chair looks like it moves electronically, it doesn't. The actor had to shuffle his feet to move the chair.

2547. The sound that Jabba makes when he opens his mouth was from the sound-operator running his hands through a casserole. In case you were wondering, it was a cheese casserole.

2548.   In the Endor scenes, Peter Mayhew was worried that he might be shot by hunters while he was wearing the Chewbacca costume.

2549.   The name "Endor" originates from an Israeli territory in the Bible.

2550.   Ian McDiarmid and Dave Prowse never met. In all of their scenes, Vader was played by Bob Anderson.

2551.   According to Ian McDiarmid, The Emperor is a hundred years old in this film. This would mean that he was seventy in Star Wars: Episode I – The Phantom Menace.

2552.   It used to take Anthony Daniels two hours to put on the C-3PO costume. In this film, it took ten minutes.

2553.   The Ewoks speak in a Fillipino language called Tagalog.

2554.   In the original script, the Ewoks were going to be Chewbacca's race, the Wookiees.

2555.   Most of the dancers in Jabba's Palace are mimes.

2556.   Ben Kingsley was nearly cast as The Emperor.

2557.   The Emperor's name, Sheev Palpatine, is never said once.

2558.   The Ewoks were originally going to be very tall and bird-like with extremely long legs.

2559.   Vader's funeral was a last-minute idea. It was so last minute that it was shot outside Lucas' house, just before the film was shipped to cinemas.

2560.   There was supposed to be a scene where Luke Skywalker takes off Vader's helmet and dons it himself to become the new Vader. Apparently, a lot of people liked the idea but Lucas hated it.

Steamboat Bill, Jr.
(1928)

2561. Even if you haven't heard of this film, you probably know of it because of one famous sequence. This film has a shot where Buster Keaton stands in front of a house that falls on top of him. However, Keaton wasn't crushed because he happened to be standing where the window was and the house fell through him and he was unharmed.

Most of the crew were so sure that he was going to be crushed, that they ran off the set, refusing to have anything to do with it.

2562. Although Charles Reisner was the director, Keaton also directed the film. Sadly, he was uncredited.

2563. The day before the house-collapsing scene, Keaton learned that his studio, United Artists, was being shut down. He was so devastated that he didn't care if the house-collapsing scene went wrong and actually crushed him.

2564. Alternative takes and camera angles were discovered of the film in 2010.

2565. Airplane propellers were used to create the cyclone effects.

2566. This film inspired Steamboat Willie, the first official Mickey Mouse cartoon.

2567. The cyclone was a flood in the original script.

2568. This film lost more money than any of Keaton's films for United Artists.

2569.   Three blocks were built to create the film's town.

2570.   This was the last film Keaton made with United
Artists. Sadly, he disappeared into obscurity and he
developed a crippling alcohol addiction.

The Sting
(1973)

2571.   Jack Nicholson turned down the role of Johnny Hooker. Robert Redford was cast in the end.

2572.   This film is based off David Maurer's novel, The Big Con.

2573.   The film is based off the real-life grifters, Charley and Fred Gondorf.

2574.   Warren Beatty was considered for Johnny.

2575.   Redford used his right hand in a weird way in some scenes because he had a broken thumb.

2576.   Robert Shaw walked with a limp because he tore the ligaments in his knee just before filming.

2577.   Julia Phillips was the film's producer. She won an Oscar for Best Picture. This was the first time a woman had been nominated and won an Oscar for Best Picture.

2578.   Paul Newman had a hand-double for the card scenes.

2579.   Lee Van Cleef was considered for the role of Henry.

2580.   Robert Redford didn't see the film until 2004.

Strangers on a Train
(1951)

2581.   Alfred Hitchcock cameoed as double bass fiddler who boards a train.

2582.   There are several references to Edgar Allen Poe throughout the story.

2583.   This film is based off Raymond Chandler's novel. Hitchcock bought the rights to the novel anonymously because he knew Chandler hated him.

2584.   This was the first successful film Hitchcock directed in four years.

2585.   Hitchcock wanted a tragic ending but the studio forced him to make a happy ending

2586.   The exploding carousel was actually a miniature.

2587.   Hitchcock personally designed the lobster claw tie Bruno wears.

2588.   Hitchcock's cameo was directed by his daughter, Patricia.

2589.   Robert Walker played Bruno. He died very suddenly after filming ended.

2590.   The scene where the man crawls under the carousel was the most dangerous stunt Hitchcock ever did.

Sunset Blvd.
(1950)

2591.   When William Holden and Nancy Olson kissed for the first time, the director didn't yell, "Cut!" He just let them kiss for ages until it felt uncomfortable.

2592.   Montgomery Clift was cast but he had to quit the production. He was having an affair with a middle-aged former actress just like his character and he was worried it would be uncovered when the media started snooping around in his private life.

2593.   Marlon Brando was up for the lead but he was dismissed for being too unknown.

2594.   Gene Kelly was considered for the lead but his studio wouldn't let him do it.

2595.   The writers worried that Hollywood would dismiss the film because it showed the film industry in a negative light. As a result, the codename for the film was "A Can of Beans."

2596.   Although Erich von Stroheim played the significant role of Max the butler, he dismissed the part as "that butler role."

2597.   Gloria Swanson played Norma Desmond. When she did the final scene, it was so perfect that the director threw a party immediately after (even though it wasn't the final scene filmed.)

2598.   Gloria Swanson burst into tears immediately after she finished her final scene.

2599.   Legendary director, Cecil B. DeMille, cameoed in the film. He is at the studio during Norma's visit.

2600.   When Billy Wilder was asked how they were going to shoot the monkey burial scene, he said, "You know, the usual monkey-funeral sequence."

Taxi Driver
(1976)

2601.   Robert De Niro's direction for the "You talkin' to me?" scene was, "Do something."

2602.   De Niro obtained a taxi driving license for this film.

2603.   De Niro did fifteen hour shifts every day for a month as a taxi driver before filming.

2604.   Paul Schrader wrote two drafts of the script in ten days.

2605.   Paul Schrader kept a loaded gun by his side while he was writing the script. He said it motivated him.

2606.   The director, Martin Scorsese, says the most important scene is when Bickle calls Betsy to get another date and the camera moves away.

2607.   Jodie Foster was twelve when she was cast.

2608.   De Niro won an Oscar for The Godfather: Part II while he was shooting this film. The studio was terrified that he would demand more money. He didn't.

2609.   Jeff Bridges was considered for the part of Travis Bickle.

2610.   Dustin Hoffman turned down the lead role.

The Terminator
(1984)

2611. When Arnold Schwarzenegger first met the director, James Cameron, Arnold said he imagined that the Terminator would be able to reload a gun without looking at it because a killing machine would be designed to be as efficient as possible. Cameron was so impressed, that he cast Arnold on the spot. Originally, Cameron was meeting him to tell him he was wrong for the part.

2612. Arnold wanted to play Kyle Reese.

2613. Lance Henriksen (Bishop from the film, Aliens) nearly played Kyle Reese.

2614. Arnold worked with guns every day for a month until he could reload a gun blindfolded.

2615. The film was delayed for nine months because Arnold was working on Conan the Destroyer. As Cameron waited, he wrote the script for Aliens.

2616. Arnold was so hungry one day, that he went into a restaurant for lunch, forgetting to take off his makeup. He looked like he was missing an eye, had an exposed jawbone and burned flesh.

2617. Bruce Willis was considered for Kyle Reese.

2618. At the start of the film, the Terminator drives over a toy semi-truck. Later, he is run over by the same model of semi-truck.

2619. Sting turned down the role of Kyle Reese.

2620.   Michael Biehn and Arnold Schwarzenegger are only in the same shot once.

2621.   Kyle Reese only smiles one time.

2622.   The Terminator kills twenty-nine people.

2623.   The crew wore shirts that said, "You can't scare me, I work for James Cameron."

2624.   It took six months to create the puppet of Arnold's face.

2625.   The voice on the answering machine near the beginning belonged to James Cameron.

2626.   Arnold avoided all of the other actors as much as possible.

2627.   Arnold's line, "I'll be back" was meant to be, "I'll come back" but he couldn't say it right.

2628.   In Poland, this film is called "The Electronic Murderer."

2629.   James Cameron was living in his car when he wrote this script.

2630.   The magazine, Soldier of Fortune, often talk about how films inaccurately portray how guns. However, they complimented Arnold, saying that everything he does with his weapons (holding, firing, reloading) was accurate.

2631.   Mel Gibson turned down the role of The Terminator.

2632. Despite what some sources say, Lance Henriksen was never considered to play the Terminator. He wore the outfit so Cameron could see how it looked when the Terminator moved.

2633. Cameron said that Mad Max 2 was a huge inspiration for this film.

2634. Arnold didn't want to say "I'll" for his "I'll be back" line because he said it sounded too casual. A robot would say "I will." However, he admitted later that he didn't want to say "I'll" because it sounded feminine.

2635. The iconic sunglasses that the Terminator wears are Gargoyles.

2636. In the original script, there were supposed to be two Terminators; a metal robot and a liquid robot. Cameron didn't have the technology to make this idea possible until the sequel.

2637. Cameron said that the television show, The Outer Limits, was a big influence on the story.

2638. Arnie based the Terminator's movements on an eagle attacking its prey.

2639. Originally, James Cameron wanted O.J. Simpson to play The Terminator. The studio rejected the idea, saying that they couldn't picture O.J. killing people.................... Moving on.

2640. Dark Horse Comics created several comic books with The Terminator looking like O.J. Simpson.

Terminator 2: Judgement Day
(1991)

2641.   Terminator 2 won four Oscars.

2642.   Robert Patrick was really insecure about his performance as the villain, the T-1000. He said some of the crew were laughing at him because they couldn't believe someone of his size could throw Arnold Schwarzenegger around a room.

2643.   Robert Patrick used to play American football until he injured his leg, causing him to have a mild limp. The director, James Cameron, liked this because it made the T-1000 move less like a human and more like a mechanism.

2644.   Edward Furlong had to redub his lines after filming because his voice broke during the shoot. However, he didn't redub the scene where he explains to the Terminator why humans cry because "it felt right."

2645.   When this film was released, Cameron wanted it to be a surprise when the audience learns that Arnold's Terminator isn't evil. However, the trailer spoiled the twist.

2646.   In the trailer, Sarah Connor asks the Terminator, "Can it be destroyed?
        He answers by saying, "Unknown."
        This isn't in the final cut.

2647.   A deleted scene shows John Connor teaching the Terminator how to smile. The scene was cut because it was too comedic, compared to the dark tone of the film.

2648.   The guard that gets stabbed in the eye by the T-1000 was played by Don Stanton. The T-1000 version of the guard was played by his twin, Dan Stanton.

2649.   The two Sarah Connors at the end of the film are played by Linda Hamilton and her twin sister, Leslie.

2650.   In the uncut version, the T-1000 starts to glitch in the final scene. This was removed because James Cameron wanted the T-1000 to seem unstoppable until the very end.

2651.   It took two weeks for Arnold to shoot the lock off a gate while driving through it on a Harley. He said it was really hard to do it "and look cool."

2652.   Arnold had to learn to cock his shotgun without looking while driving a motorcycle. He did it so many times that he tore the skin off his fingers. He said it was extremely painful but he wasn't allowed to wear a glove because the Terminator wouldn't need one.

2653.   When the T-1000 is driving the helicopter, you can very briefly see that he has three hands. Two hands are reloading the gun while a third hand is driving the helicopter.

2654.   A scene of Miles Dyson talking to his wife was cut. It was supposed to show that the man who would be responsible for Judgement Day was a normal, loving man. However, Cameron thought this fact would be more significant if the audience learned it at the same time as Sarah Connor when she was about to kill him.

2655.   Sarah Connor complains that certain parts of the steel mill are "too hot." Ironically, the steel mill was extremely cold.

2656. When the T-1000 moves through a crowd, his movements are based off a shark moving in on its prey.

2657. James Cameron cast Robert Patrick for the T-1000 after seeing him in Die Hard 2.

2658. In the playground dream sequence, the child that Sarah Connor is playing with is played by Dalton, Linda Hamilton's son.

2659. Linda Hamilton suffered permanent hearing loss from the elevator scene near the end.

2660. Linda Hamilton had to train with a former Israeli commando called Uzi Gal to learn how to use guns.

2661. Linda Hamilton trained three hours a day, six days a week for thirteen weeks before filming.

2662. This was Edward Furlong's film debut.

2663. When the Terminator shoots his shotgun, the sound effect is actually two cannons.

2664. When the Terminator tells Sarah Connor about Miles Dyson, he is reading his dialogue from a card on the car's windshield.

2665. The Terminators in the film's intro weren't just puppets. They were fully operational animatronics.

2666. Arnold was paid $15 million for this film. He only speaks 700 words throughout the film. That means that he got paid $21,429 per word.

2667.   This is the only sequel to win an Oscar when the previous film wasn't even nominated.

2668.   The biker bar scene was shot the same night Rodney King was beaten by the police. Bizarrely, the bar was right across where the beating occurred.

2669.   James Cameron cameos as the biker in the bar that drops the pool stick.

2670.   A woman walked into the biker bar, believing it was a real bar. When she asked why Arnold was only wearing boxer shorts, he said, "It's male stripper night."

There Will Be Blood
(2007)

2671.   Russell Harvard plays Plainview's deaf son as a young man. Harvard is actually deaf.

2672.   Daniel Day-Lewis won an Oscar for Best Actor for this film. He dedicated his award to Heath Ledger.

2673.   Day-Lewis said that he played his character, Daniel Plainview, as an asexual.

2674.   Plainview's voice is based off John Huston.

2675.   An actor quit because he found Day-Lewis too intimidating.

2676.   Day-Lewis ad-libbed the "building schools" speech.

2677.   The director believed that the film wouldn't have been made if Day-Lewis turned it down.

2678.   Paul Dano was only supposed to play Paul Sunday. The director, Paul Thomas Anderson, decided to make Paul and his brother, Eli, twins at the last minute.

2679.   Day-Lewis is a Method actor, which means he lives as the character he is portraying. To help him maintain this, the director and crew would eat steak and vodka with him, as that is what his character would have eaten in that time.

2680.   Day-Lewis didn't tell Paul Dano that he was going to hurl bowling balls at him in the Milkshake scene. When one ball nearly hit Dano, he broke character and screamed, "Daniel! STOP!"

However, Daniel Day-Lewis' character was also called Daniel so it didn't ruin the shot and it captured genuine terror in Dano's face. This was the shot used for the final cut.

The Thing
(1982)

2681. The film is based off the John Campbell's novel, Who Goes There?

2682. John Carpenter directed this film. This is the film that he is most proud of.

2683. There are two characters called Mac and Windows. Coincidentally, these names are now associated with computers.

2684. The film has one of the greatest film posters ever. It was drawn by legendary artist, Drew Struzan. Struzan is famous for drawing the posters for all of the Star Wars and Indiana Jones films. Struzan had no idea what the alien in the film looked like so he created the poster as best he could. Carpenter loved it.

2685. The film's poster was done in one attempt in a single night.

2686. Keith David wears gloves because he broke his hand before filming and he had to hide his cast.

2687. This film was banned in Finland.

2688. Nick Nolte was considered for a role.

2689. Jeff Bridges turned down a role.

2690. The final battle with the Thing required fifty technicians.

The Third Man
(1949)

2691.   Orson Welles played Harry Lime. Lime isn't the lead part so it was odd for the audience to see a big star playing a small part. It was this film that popularised famous actors playing smaller roles.

2692.   Harry Lime has a famous monologue where he says the only thing that Switzerland ever made was the cuckoo clock. This is untrue. The cuckoo clock originated from Germany.

2693.   Orson Welles is only in the film for five minutes.

2694.   Although the film takes place in Vienna and was always considered a classic, it didn't do well in Austria.

2695.   The film was surprisingly successful in the UK at the time of its release.

2696.   Cary Grant was considered for the part of Harry Lime.

2697.   Noel Coward was the first choice to play Harry Lime.

2698.   Welles was certain he would capture a disease in the sewer scene and refused to do it at first.

2699.   Martin Scorsese wrote a thesis on it while he was in film school. His teacher said, "Forget it, it's just a thriller."

2700.   Welles only worked for one week on the film.

This is Spinal Tap
(1984)

2701. In Norway, the film is called "Help! We are in the Pop Business!"

2702. According to the band members, they have had thirty-two drummers and all of them died in thirty-two freak accidents.

2703. Many people thought Spinal Tap was a genuine band for years after this film was released.

2704. Ozzy Osbourne thought the film was a real documentary.

2705. All of the actors in Spinal Tap are actually played their instruments and used their own voices. There was no dubbing over.

2706. Billy Crystal and Dana Carvey cameo as mime waiters.

2707. Rob Reiner's character is called Marty DiBergi. His name is an homage to Martin Scorsese, Brian De Palma, Steven Spielberg and Federico Fellini.

2708. Spinal Tap appeared in The Simpsons. Harry Shearer played the Spinal Tap member, Derek Smalls. He plays many recurring characters in The Simpsons such as Mr. Burns, Smithers and Flanders.

2709. Most of the dialogue is ad-libbed.

2710. This is the only film on IMDB that is rated out of 11.

To Kill a Mockingbird
(1962)

2711.   When Gregory Peck was offered the part of Atticus Finch, he bough Harper Lee's novel, To Kill a Mockingbird. He read the entire book in one sitting.

2712.   Brock Peters played Tom Robinson, the man who Finch defends. When Gregory Peck died, his eulogy was performed by Brock Peters.

2713.   This was the film debut of Robert Duvall. He had no dialogue.

2714.   The director used very few takes for the children. He noticed that the more takes they had, the less spontaneous they acted.

2715.   Duvall plays a recluse. To prepare for the part, Duvall avoided the sun for six weeks.

2716.   This was the film that Peck was proudest of.

2717.   In the Superman comics, this is Clark Kent's favourite film.

2718.   James Earl Jones auditioned for the role of Tom Robinson.

2719.   Eight actors in this film have starred in Star Trek.

2720.   Gregory Peck's court speech was nine minutes long. He did it in one take.

Touch of Evil
(1958)

2721.   The opening shot took all night to do. It was a long take, involving dozens of props and vehicles and hundreds of actors and had to be done in one shot. Unfortunately, the actor who played the customs officer kept messing up his line. As the sun was beginning to rise, the director, Orson Welles, realised that they had minutes to get the shot. Welles went up to the actor and said, "If you forget your line this time, just move your lips and we'll dub it in later." The next take was the one they used for the final cut.

2722.   Welles became the director due to a misunderstanding. He thought he was supposed to act in the film and nothing else. When he was told that he had to also direct, he accepted it and rewrote the script. Due to disagreements with the studio, he was fired as the director weeks later.

2723.   Welles shot at night to avoid producers storming on set, complaining about how he was directing the film.

2724.   Zsa Zsa Gabor demanded that she had a title card for the film that said, "Guest Starring Zsa Zsa Gabor." She was in the film for twenty seconds.

2725.   Welles was a very good-looking man who became very heavy in his later life. Many people believe this was the film where Welles began to pile on the pounds. However, Welles looks large in this film because he was wearing 70lbs of body prosthetics and a fake nose.

2726.   Until he got fired, Welles said this was the most fun he had making a film.

2727.   Orson Welles hated the title.

2728.   When Welles was fired, the film was recut. He wrote a letter to the studio, detailing how the film should be directed but his instructions were ignored. The film was recut according to Welles instructions in 1998 (thirteen years after he died.) This version is now considered to be the definitive film and is vastly superior than the original cut.

2729.   Welles called the first cut "an odious thing" and wanted nothing to do with it.

2730.   The film was going to be called "Borderline."

Toy Story
(1995)

2731.   When PIXAR decided to make a film made entirely out of computer-generated images, they had to brainstorm what the story would be. They tried to create human characters but the animation wasn't good enough yet and the humans looked blocky and had rigid movements. PIXAR also realised that their technology wasn't good enough to create human hair. One animator pointed out that their human characters moved like toy soldiers. Also, hair wasn't a problem for toys because characters like Woody have "set" hair that doesn't move or change. This was what inspired the idea to make a film about toys. Toy Story only exists because of the limitations of the technology of the time.

2732.   Chevy Chase was considered for the part of Buzz Lightyear.

2733.   Paul Newman was considered for Woody.

2734.   In 2013, Jonason Pauley recreated the film shot-for-shot with actual toys and real people. It took him two years to complete.

2735.   The carpets in Sid's house have the same pattern as the hotel carpet in the film, The Shining.

2736.   The Woody doll in real life is voiced by Tom Hanks brother, Jim.

2737.   Joss Whedon created the character, Rex the Dinosaur.

2738.   The original title was "You Are a Toy."

2739.   This was the most successful film of 1995.

2740.   Billy Crystal turned down Buzz Lightyear.

Toy Story 2
(1999)

2741.   In the last few years, a rumour circulated the Internet suggesting that Jessie's owner is actually Andy's mom. The director confirmed that this is true.

2742.   This film nearly went straight to DVD.

2743.   Tom Hanks said he cried the first time saw he saw the scene where Jessie sings.

2744.   When Jessie meets Woody, she says, "Sweet mother of Abraham Lincoln!" Lincoln is a distant relative of Tom Hanks, the actor who plays Woody.

2745.   John Ratzenberger played Hamm. He plays a character in every PIXAR film.

2746.   The hardest part of the film to animate was the dust in the scene with Wheezy.

2747.   When this was reviewed on rottentomatoes.com, it had the highest rating of any film ever.

2748.   Zurg's planet is called Xrghthung.

2749.   Zurg is voiced by the film's writer, Andrew Stanton. He also directed WALL-E and Finding Nemo.

2750.   90% of the film was deleted by accident! Luckily, the technical director made a copy of the film (without anyone's permission) to show to her kids. When the film was deleted, she had the only copy. When it was brought into the office, the animators said that they only lost a week of work. If she didn't make a copy, it's very likely that the film would have never been made.

Toy Story 3
(2010)

2751.   Lotso actually appears in the first Toy Story. He appears in the staff meeting when Woody asks if the toys "up on the shelf can hear."

2752.   Tim Allen and Tom Hanks recorded their lines together. This is incredibly rare for animated films.

2753.   A lot of babies auditioned for the part of Big Baby. The baby that got the part is called Woody.

2754.   Jim Varney played Slinky Dog in the first two films. Sadly, he died before this film began production. He was replaced by Blake Clark.

2755.   The hardest thing to animate in this film was the trash bags.

2756.   Ken wears twenty-one outfits.

2757.   Chuckles appears in the first Toy Story on the "last present" as wrapping paper.

2758.   It took two-and-a-half years to write the script.

2759.   The Jack in the Box is voiced by the director, Lee Unkrich.

2760.   The bin-man is Sid from the first film.

Trainspotting
(1996)

2761.   Ewan McGregor strongly considered using heroin to understand his character better.

2762.   A prosthetic arm was created for the scene when Renton injects himself.

2763.   Ewan McGregor lost 30lbs for his character.

2764.   Johnny Lee Miller is the only main actor that wasn't Scottish.

2765.   Most shots were done in one take.

2766.   Ewen Bremner played Spud. He played the lead character, Renton, in the stage adaptation of the novel.

2767.   Christopher Eccleston was offered the part of Begbie.

2768.   Renton's dealer is played by Irvine Welsh, the writer of the novel.

2769.   Robert Carlyle couldn't get work for years because everyone thought he was a lunatic after his performance as Begbie. He said that people crossed the street to avoid him almost every day.

2770.   Carlyle said that he played Begbie as a repressed homosexual and that is why he is so angry all of the time. Weirdly, this is exactly how the writer, Irvine Welsh, intended the character to be.

The Treasure of the Sierra Madre
(1948)

2771.　Humphrey Bogart was completely bald by the time film production began. He had to wear a wig for the film.

2772.　The director, John Huston, wrote the part of Howard for his father.

2773.　John Huston cameos as an American tourist.

2774.　The Mexican extras were paid the equivalent of $2 a day. This was actually considered a lot at the time.

2775.　This is Robert Redford's favourite film.

2776.　The cantina fight took five days to shoot.

2777.　Humphrey Bogart directed one scene.

2778.　Ronald Reagan was considered for a part.

2779.　Sam Peckinpah said this film inspired him to make many films, especially The Wild Bunch.

2780.　It took nearly six months to shoot the film.

The Truman Show
(1998)

2781.   Truman's wife, Meryl, has a bottle of vitamin D. All of the "actors" on the show have to take it since they can't be exposed to the real sun.

2782.   The film takes place over five days.

2783.   It took $75,000 to make the film's poster.

2784.   Dennis Hopper was supposed to play Christof.

2785.   Truman's boat is the Santa Maria, the same name as Christopher Columbus' ship. Both men sought to explore "a new world."

2786.   Gary Oldman auditioned for Truman.

2787.   Sam Raimi nearly directed the film.

2788.   David Cronenberg turned down directing duties.

2789.   In the original script, all of the Truman actors were criminals. They had to act in the show to avoid jail.

2790.   Ed Harris and Jim Carrey never met throughout filming.

Twelve Monkeys
(1995)

2791.   Brad Pitt said that all he had to do to play the insane Jeffrey Goines was stop smoking.

2792.   The director, Terry Gilliam, gave Bruce Willis a list of "acting clichés" he was not allowed to use in this film.

2793.   Although it is never said in the film, the future scenes take place in 2035.

2794.   The tagline was supposed to be, "The future is in the hands of a man who has none." It was dropped as some people thought this meant that the character had no hands.

2795.   Test screenings went terribly for the film. However, Gilliam changed nothing about the film and released it anyway. It went on to be a huge success.

2796.   This was the first film that Gilliam had final cut of.

2797.   The Army of the Twelve Monkeys was inspired by L. Frank Baum's novel, The Magic of Oz. It is a sequel to The Wizard of Oz.

2798.   Johnny Depp was considered for Goines.

2799.   The film was inspired by the 1962 short, La Jetee.

2800.   At the time of filming, Terry Gilliam hadn't seen La Jetee, even though it inspired the story.

2801.   Brad Pitt was an unknown actor when he got cast. He was one of the biggest stars in Hollywood when the film was released.

2802.   Jeff Bridges was considered for the lead.

2803.   Gilliam nearly died in a horse-riding accident during the film's production.

2804.   Pitt won his first Golden Globe for the film.

2805.   The virus is released on Friday, December 13th 1996.

2806.   Kathryn puts on a blonde wig while she watches a Hitchcock film. Hitchcock usually cast a blonde woman in his films.

2807.   The final scene takes place in an airport. It was shot in two different airports.

2808.   Gilliam wanted Nick Nolte to play Cole.

2809.   Some scenes were shot in an actual prison. It was the Eastern State Penitentiary in Philadelphia, the world's first penitentiary ever built.

2810.   When Cole is drawing blood from himself, there is a shadow of a hamster in a hamster wheel. Gilliam wanted the hamster to run in his wheel but it refused to. It took Gilliam all day to make the hamster run in the wheel. This detail is almost impossible to notice in the finished film but Gilliam became well known for his perfectionism after this. There is even a documentary about it called The Hamster Factor that you can watch on YouTube.

Unforgiven
(1992)

2811.   Clint Eastwood's mother plays an extra. Her scene was cut.

2812.   The film was supposed to be shot in forty-four days. It was shot in thirty-nine. Clint Eastwood has a reputation for making his films ahead of schedule.

2813.   Clint Eastwood intended this to be the last film he would direct and act in.

2814.   Gene Hackman was worried that the film would glorify guns.

2815.   This script floated around Hollywood for twenty years.

2816.   Eastwood had the script for years but didn't read it because his script reader said it was dreadful.

2817.   No vehicles were allowed on set.

2818.   Richard Harris was watching a western when he got cast.

2819.   The boots Eastwood wears are the same ones he wore in the film, Rawhide.

2820.   This is the third western to win an Oscar for Best Picture.

The Untouchables
(1987)

2821. Bob Hoskins was originally cast as Al Capone. However, when Robert De Niro became interested in the role, the director, Brian De Palma, had to pay Bob Hoskins not to take the part. Hoskins then asked De Palma if there were any other films that the director did not want him to be in.

2822. De Niro tracked down Al Capone's tailor so he could get his suit exactly like Capone's.

2823. De Niro wore the exact same silk underwear as Capone, even though it's never seen.

2824. De Niro's scenes were the last to be shot.

2825. In real life, Capone never attempted to kill the Untouchables. He made it a strict rule that his men were not allowed to lay a finger on Ness or his men.

2826. Eliot Ness wasn't considered a significant player in taking down Al Capone. Even when Ness died, nothing in the media was mentioned about his accomplishments against Capone. Only when The Untouchables book was released, was Ness considered the person most responsible for taking down Capone.

2827. Al Capone and Eliot Ness never met each other in real life.

2828. Mickey Rourke turned down the part of Ness.

2829. Michael Douglas nearly played Ness.

2830. Harrison Ford was considered for a role.

Up
(2009)

2831. This is the first Disney film to reference infertility.

2832. This was the first film to ever be nominated for an Oscar for Best Picture and Best Animated Feature.

2833. Carl's face is based off Spencer Tracey.

2834. Carl's voice is based off Walter Matthau.

2835. The dogs literally take part in a dogfight (airplane battle) at the end.

2836. The film's codename was "Helium."

2837. Jordan Nagai plays Russell. This was his film debut.

2838. Carl is never seen speaking to his wife.

2839. Muntz has the same sword William Wallace had in the film, Braveheart.

2840. The villain, Charles Muntz, is named after Charlie Mintz; the man who stole Walt Disney's first creation, Oswald the Lucky Rabbit. Disney countered this by creating Mickey Mouse.

The Usual Suspects
(1995)

2841.   The line-up scene was supposed to be completely serious. However, none of the actors could hold a straight face, which infuriated the director. This was kept in the final cut of the film.

2842.   Kevin Spacey had his fingers on his left hand glued together.

2843.   Spacey had to consult several doctors on how cerebral palsy could effect the psychology of a person.

2844.   Keyser Soze is based off a real killer called John List. List killed his family and then vanished for seventeen years.

2845.   "Keyser" means "emperor."

2846.   Michael Biehn nearly played McManus. The part went to Stephen Baldwin.

2847.   Stephen Baldwin and Kevin Pollack despised each other throughout production. It is unknown why.

2848.   Kevin Spacey filed down his shoes to make them look worn down by his limp.

2849.   The detective that interrogates Verbal was nearly played by Christopher Walken.

2850.   Charlie Sheen was considered for the role of Redfoot.

2851.   Roger Ebert hated this film.

2852. Keyser Soze always shoots twice when he kills someone.

2853. The stolen emeralds were real gems. They were lent to the filmmakers.

2854. The writer, Christopher McQuarrie, got the name "Keyser Soze" from a Turkish dictionary.

2855. Verbal is the only one not seen getting arrested for the line up.

2856. Five people play Keyser Soze at some point in the film. This was to hide the real Keyser Soze. Even the director played him in one scene.

2857. SPOILER – After the premier, Gabriel Byrne had a huge argument with the director, Bryan Singer, because Byrne believed he was Keyser Soze for the whole film.

2858. SPOILER – Bryan Singer made each of the main cast where Keyser Soze's hat and coat without explanation. He did this because if multiple actors told their friends and family that they were Keyser Soze, it would heighten the film's twist.

2859. SPOILER – Verbal uses his "disabled arm" when Detective Kujan shoves him."

2860. SPOILER- When Verbal falls to the ground, he says, "I did it, I did kill Keaton." Detective Kujan doesn't hear him and he then covers up his slip up and says, "I did see Keaton get shot."

Vertigo
(1958)

2861.   It was supposed to be called "Fear and Trembling."

2862.   When the lead actress, Kim Novak, asked Hitchcock about the meaning of the film, he said, "It's only a movie."

2863.   Audrey Hepburn was interested in playing Judy.

2864.   James Stewart's character, Scottie, doesn't suffer from vertigo. He has a fear of heights. Vertigo is a condition that destabilises a person's equilibrium.

2865.   Hitchcock told everyone that his wife hated the film, even though she didn't. She didn't like one shot and Hitchcock took it to heart.

2866.   In 2012, this was considered to be the greatest film of all time according to the Sight & Sound critic's poll.

2867.   The word "vertigo" is only said once.

2868.   Hitchcock cameos as a man in the shipyard carrying a musical instrument case.

2869.   This was the last film Hitchcock worked on with Stewart.

2870.   The film was a flop upon its release. Hitchcock assumed the film failed because Stewart was too old to play a leading man.

WALL-E
(2008)

2871.   EVE solves a Rubik's Cube in four seconds. The world record is 5.5 seconds.

2872.   AUTO was inspired by HAL 9000 from 2001: A Space Odyssey.

2873.   The film's code name was "Sundaye."

2874.   The original plot involved green aliens kidnapping EVE.

2875.   In an early draft, the writers considered making the humans speak a new language.

2876.   Sigourney Weaver plays the Ship's Computer. This is the third time she has voiced a spaceship computer. She voiced the ship in the animated series, Futurama and the film, Galaxy Quest.

2877.   WALL-E only says EVE's name correctly twice.

2878.   The first human dialogue begins thirty-nine minutes into the film.

2879.   The last piece of space junk that you can see as WALL-E leave's Earth's orbit is Sputnik 1, the first satellite in space.

2880.   To make the ruined world look realistic, the art director studied images from Chernobyl.

Warrior
(2011)

2881.   The day before Tom Hardy's audition, he went straight to the director's door and told him to that there was no point auditioning other actors because no one is going to play the part as well as him. He got the part, then and there.

2882.   Tom Hardy lived with the director for five days.

2883.   Tom Hardy broke his toe, ribs and finger while he was choreographing his fight scenes.

2884.   The character, Koba, is described as an Olympic Gold medallist. He is played by the Olympic Gold medallist, Kurt Angle.

2885.   Koba is a Sambo fighter. Sambo focuses on leg locks. The actor, Angle's, speciality is leg locks.

2886.   Koba was supposed to be called King Kong but his name was changed for legal reasons.

2887.   Koba is based off Heavyweight Mixed Martial Arts fighter, Fedor Emelianenko.

2888.   There's an Indian remake of this film called "Brothers."

2889.   Joel Edgerton's character is based off UFC fighter, Rich "Ace" Franklin.

2890.   The character, Paddy, was written for Nick Nolte.

Whiplash
(2014)

2891. The writer and director, Damien Chazelle, couldn't get funding for the film so he made it into a short in 2013. It was met with much praise and he was given the money to make it into a feature.

2892. The entire film was shot in nineteen days.

2893. J.K. Simmons won forty-seven awards for his depiction as Fletcher.

2894. When Miles Teller tacked J.K. Simmons, Simmons cracked two of his ribs.

2895. Miles Teller has been playing the drums since he was fifteen.

2896. Teller had to drum for four hours a day, three days a week for the film.

2897. J.K. Simmons actually slapped Miles Teller in the Dragger scene.

2898. Andrew says his idol is the drummer, Buddy Rich. Buddy Rich had no music training and he said he never practised.

2899. Damien Chazelle got into a car accident during filming.

2900. This is one of the lowest grossing films ever to be nominated for a Best Picture Oscar.

Who's Afraid of Virginia Woolf?
(1966)

2901. The title is referencing the song, "Who's Afraid of the Big Bad Wolf?" However, the film couldn't get permission to sing that song so when the characters sing, "Who's afraid of Virginia Woolf?" they had to sing in a generic tune.

2902. This was the first film ever to have the rating, "No one under 18 will be admitted unless accompanied by his parent."

2903. Elizabeth Taylor gained 30lbs for her part.

2904. Virginia Woolf's novel, To the Lighthouse, is visible on a bookshelf.

2905. Jack Lemmon nearly played George.

2906. Robert Redford turned down the part of Nick.

2907. Elizabeth Taylor was thirty-three when she played the fifty-two-year-old Martha.

2908. Martha was nearly played by Bette Davis.

2909. The director, Mike Nichols, fired the First Assistant Director on the first day. He did this to establish his authority.

2910. Every actor received an Oscar nomination.

The Wild Bunch
(1969)

2911. There were so few uniforms for the film that when an extra was shot dead, that uniform would have to be repaired, taped and painted over to get rid of the blood and bullet wound so it could be used on another actor.

2912. Charlton Heston was considered for the lead.

2913. The director, Sam Peckinpah, said his main objective was to make the audience feel "what it is like to be gunned down."

2914. John Wayne despised this film.

2915. James Stewart turned down the lead.

2916. Ernest Borgnine's limp was genuine because he broke his foot before filming.

2917. "Mapache" is Spanish for "raccoon."

2918. The budget was supposed to be $3.5 million but it nearly doubled to $6 million.

2919. The director, Sam Peckinpah, said the violence in Bonnie and Clyde inspired him to make this film.

2920. 90,000 bullets were fired during production. That's more bullets than the entire Mexican Revolution of 1916.

Witness for the Prosecution
(1957)

2921.   Alfred Hitchcock said that people kept congratulating him for the film even though he didn't make it. It was directed by Billy Wilder.

2922.   This film is based off the Agatha Christie story, Traitor's Hands.

2923.   The script that the actors were given was missing the last ten pages.

2924.   Una O' Connor and Elsa Lanchester star in this film. They also starred in the Bride of Frankenstein.

2925.   Charles Laughton and Elsa Lanchester star in the film. They were husband and wife in real life.

2926.   Marlene Dietrich was so adamant that she was going to win an Oscar that she told everybody she was nominated. She wasn't.

2927.   The cast didn't know the twist until the last day of shooting.

2928.   Charles Laughton's character, Wilfrid, is recovering from a heart attack. He once faked a heart attack in public to see if he could make it look convincing. It was.

2929.   In the story, the heart-attack sufferer, Wilfrid is defending a man called Vole. Vole is played by Tyrone Power. Ironically, Power died from a heart attack after he finished filming.

2930.   At previews, audience members had to sign a card that said, "I solemnly swear I will not reveal the ending of Witness for the Prosecution."

The Wizard of Oz
(1939)

2931.   This film is based off the L. Frank Baum novel, The Wonderful Wizard of Oz. In the novel, the ruby slippers are silver.

2932.   This film is a remake of the 1925 version of The Wizard of Oz.

2933.   The Wizard's name is Professor Marvel.

2934.   The song, Over the Rainbow, was nearly cut from the film.

2935.   A lot of the Wicked Witch's scenes were shortened or cut because the director thought audiences would find her too scary.

2936.   Judy Garland had to wear a corset so she would look younger. She said it was very painful to wear.

2937.   There is an urban legend that a Munchkin hung himself and you can see his hanging body in the scene before the Tin Man, the Scarecrow and Dorothy meet the Cowardly Lion. With HD quality television, viewers can see this "hanging body" is a crane bird.

2938.   The lion costume weighed 90lbs.

2939.   When the Wicked Witch tries to touch the ruby slippers, fire shoots out of them. This special effect was done by having apple juice spraying out of the shoes and then speeding up the footage to top speed.

2940. When smoke appears after the Wicked Witch leaves Munchkinland, the actress, Margaret Hamilton, suffered third-degree burns.

2941. The green horses of Oz were painted with Jell-O.

2942. Dorothy never says, "Toto, I have a feeling we're not in Kansas anymore." She says, "We're not in Kansas anymore, Toto."

2943. The dog that plays Toto is called Terry. She has starred in eighteen films.

2944. Although Terry was the main dog to play Toto, she had two stunt doubles.

2945. The actors who played the Munchkins were paid $50 per week.

2946. Terry the dog earned $125 per week.

2947. Ray Bolger was cast as the Tin Man but he convinced the director to cast him as the Scarecrow.

2948. The director, Richard Thorpe, was fired and replaced after two weeks.

2949. Everybody that worked on this film said it was an absolute nightmare to shoot.

2950. The Head flying monkey is called Nikko.

2951. Judy Garland wore a blonde wig as Dorothy for the first few weeks.

2952. The writer, Baum, came up with the name of Oz when he looked at a filing cabinet that said A-N and O-Z.

2953.   The sequel, Return to Oz, was released in 1985. At the time, it had the world record for the longest time between a film and its sequel – forty-six years.

2954.   The "snow" in the Poppy Field scene was made of asbestos. At the time of filming, it was common knowledge that asbestos was potentially lethal.

2955.   The Wicked Witch never says, "Fly my pretties, fly" to the monkeys. She simply says, "Fly, fly, fly."

2956.   The makeup that Ray Bolger wore as the Scarecrow left lines on his face that didn't fade for over a year.

2957.   The Witch's castle guards are called Winkies.

2958.   The film involved fourteen writers and five directors.

2959.   Shirley Temple was considered for the lead role.

2960.   Judy Garland breaks character in the scene where she meets the Lion. After he says, "Is my nose bleeding?" she replies with, "No, of course not." You can see her hiding her laughter with Toto for a second before she continues the scene.

The Wolf of Wall Street
(2013)

2961. This was the first film Jonah Hill auditioned for six years.

2962. Margot Robbie slapped Leonardo DiCaprio during her audition, even though it wasn't in the script. After she did it, she was certain she ruined her chances of getting the part.

2963. The snorted cocaine is actually crushed Vitamin B tablets.

2964. A lot of the dialogue was improvised.

2965. Jonah Hill was so desperate to work with Martin Scorsese, that he was paid the minimum amount he was entitled to - $60,000.

2966. Matthew McConnaughey's chest-beating is something the actor actually does to warm up before a scene.

2967. The scene where DiCaprio's character, Jordan Belfort, has to crawl towards his car was DiCaprio's idea. It was shot in one take.

2968. This is the most successful film Martin Scorsese has ever made.

2969. Scorsese believes that Jordon Belfort is the most despicable character in all of his films (and that's saying a lot.)

2970. Chris Evans was considered for the lead.

2971. Joseph Gordon-Levitt auditioned for the part of Jordon Belfort.

2972. Rosie Huntington-Whiteley was considered for Naomi.

2973. Blake Lively auditioned for the part of Naomi.

2974. The character, Steve Madden, is played by Jake Hoffman, Dustin Hoffman's son.

2975. The first cut of the film was four hours.

2976. Jordon Belfort appears as the man who introduces DiCaprio in the final scene.

2977. Ridley Scott nearly directed this film.

2978. In the improvisation scenes, Martin Scorsese's rule was, "Don't say anything important."

2979. This is the longest film Scorsese has directed.

2980. Some of the scenes intentionally have bad continuity so the audience will see the scenes in the same confusing manner as the drug-addicted characters.

The Wrestler
(2008)

2981.   Nicholas Cage was supposed to play the lead role. The director, Darren Aronofsky, eventually realised that he wasn't suited to the character and had him replaced with Mickey Rourke. When Nicholas Cage saw the film, he told Aronofsky that he made the right decision.

2982.   The pictures of the Ram in his prime are photoshopped images of former WWF wrestler, Lex Luger.

2983.   In the wrestling entertainment business, wrestlers will cut themselves in the forehead with a concealed blade to draw a lot of blood to emphasise an injury. This practice is known as blading. Mickey Rourke actually did this for the film.

2984.   Recently deceased wrestler, Roddy Piper, cried when he saw the film because he believed it captured the depressing lifestyle of a wrestler perfectly.

2985.   The budget was so tight that Axl Rose donated his Guns N' Roses song free of charge.

2986.   Mickey Rourke wasn't paid for this film.

2987.   Marisa Tomei's first day of shooting required her to give Mickey Rourke a lap dance.

2988.   There is less than thirteen minutes of wrestling in the film.

2989.   Sylvester Stallone was considered for the lead.

2990.   Mark Margolis has appeared in this film as well as every film Aronofsky has directed. He is more well known for playing the invalid, Salamanca, in Breaking Bad.

Yojimbo
(1961)

2991. "Yojimbo" means "bodyguard" in Japanese.

2992. Toshiro Mifune plays the lead, Sanjuro. He based his character off the movements of a dog.

2993. The sound effect of a sword slicing is of two wooden chopsticks in a raw chicken being hacked with a blade.

2994. The wind represents the chaos of the town.

2995. The dust was created by a wind machine blasting into a truckload full of dust.

2996. The dust scene made one actor suffer hives for weeks.

2997. Some of the film takes elements from the Dashiell Hammett novel, The Glass Key.

2998. Yojimbo is based off the Hammett novel, Red Harvest.

2999. Yojimbo was remade into the western, A Fistful of Dollars. The western was sued for blatantly stealing the story of Yojimbo.

3000. Tatsuya Nakadai plays the character Unosuke. He plays the villain in the sequel, Sanjuro.

Printed in Great Britain
by Amazon